Inevitable Imposter

Identify and Defeat Imposter Syndrome

© 2025 Philip B. Terry-Smith, Ph.D., ThD.

Inevitable Imposter
© 2025 Philip B. Terry-Smith, Ph.D., ThD

ISBN 978-0-9885429-9-0
www.coachpositive.com
www.drpterrysmith.com
Marcey Creek Publishing

Contents

WHAT MAKES YOU FEEL LEGIT? 1

WHAT IS IMPOSTER SYNDROME? 3
WHO SUFFERS FROM IMPOSTER SYNDROME? 11
HOW IMPOSTER SYNDROME HOLDS US BACK 14
AM I AN IMPOSTER? 16
THE VARIOUS TYPES OF "IMPOSTERS" 16
IMPOSTER SYNDROME SELF-TEST 26

DEALING WITH IMPOSTER SYNDROME 33

TECHNIQUES FOR DEALING WITH IMPOSTER SYNDROME 33

KEEPING IMPOSTER SYNDROME AWAY FOR GOOD 45

WRAP UP 50

ELIMINATING SELF DEFEATING BEHAVIORS 51

WHAT SELF-DEFEATING HABITS ARE 53
COMMON SELF-DEFEATING BEHAVIORS 54

HOW SELF-DEFEATING BEHAVIORS ARE FORMED 69

CAUSES OF CURRENT SELF-SABOTAGE INCLUDE: 72
CHASING SATISFACTION OUTSIDE OF YOURSELF 83

HOW TO ELIMINATE SELF-DEFEATING BEHAVIORS 85

Wrap up 94

SOLVING YOUR SELF-DEFEATING BEHAVIOR: CHECKLIST .. 96

INEVITABLE 98

DEVELOPING AN UNWAVERING BELIEF IN YOUR DECISIONS AND ACTIONS 98

IT'S INEVITABLE? 99
- What is Self-Belief? 101
- Why Do We Lack Self-Belief? 103

WHAT HAPPENS WHEN WE DON'T BELIEVE IN OURSELVES? 108

A Quick Self-Test 116

THE POWER OF SELF-BELIEF 119

THE BENEFITS OF UNWAVERING BELIEF IN OUR DECISIONS 124
- The Decision-Making Process 125

THE BENEFITS OF UNWAVERING BELIEF IN OUR ACTIONS 130

INEVITABLE: DEVELOPING UNWAVERING BELIEF 133
- Wrap up 146

THE NEW YOU: THE 7 POINT ATTITUDE ADJUSTMENT TO CHANGE YOUR LIFE 148

iii

INTRODUCTION 148

THE NEGATIVE ATTITUDE 151

THE POSITIVE ATTITUDE 159
POSITIVE ATTITUDE AND YOUR HEALTH 162
BENEFITS OF A POSITIVE ATTITUDE 164

THE 7 POINT ATTITUDE ADJUSTMENT 167
THINK POSITIVE THOUGHTS 168
CREATE YOUR HAPPINESS 171
BOOST YOUR PERSONAL ENERGY 174
BELIEVE IN YOURSELF 177
WORRY LESS 179
CONQUER YOUR FEARS 182
OVERCOME NEGATIVITY IN OTHERS 185

SELF ACCEPTANCE 189
WHAT IS SELF-ACCEPTANCE? 191
WHY ACCEPTING YOURSELF IS SO CHALLENGING 193

9 WAYS TO BEGIN ACCEPTING YOURSELF 198
SELF-ESTEEM AND SELF-CONFIDENCE 203
MEDITATION AS A TOOL FOR SELF-ACCEPTANCE 206

DEVELOPING SELF-AWARENESS 212

WHAT TO LOOK FOR WHILE DEVELOPING SELF-AWARENESS
.... 220

BE AWARE OF YOUR MOTIVATIONS 222

WHAT IS YOUR PERSONALITY TYPE? 223

HOW TO FLEX YOUR FLEXIBILITY MUSCLE 226

IMPORTANCE OF APPRECIATION 231
UNITY CONSCIOUSNESS 232

ACKNOWLEDGE YOUR NEGATIVE TRAITS 236

PERCEPTION IS THE KEY 237

USING SELF-AWARENESS TO BE YOUR BEST SELF 239

KEEP A JOURNAL 245

WAYS TO DEVELOP SELF-AWARENESS 246
CONCLUSION 249

What makes you feel legit?

As children, we're taught to look for approval from those around us. This approval is how we learn when we're doing things the right way. We beam with pride when we're praised and complimented, to the point where it becomes quite natural to keep your eye on others as a means of figuring out if you're on the right track.

The problem with outside validation is it undermines our confidence. At some point, we don't get the feedback we want or even deserve, and after a while, we might even come to think we're no good at things we excel at simply because no one has given us the feedback we needed.

Now, imposter syndrome starts to bloom.

The problem is, we're not in the habit of validating ourselves. We don't always take the time to recognize our accomplishments, so we start thinking we don't have them. We might even become convinced we don't know what we're doing at all.

Welcome to the world of Imposter Syndrome.

This book will find out more about what Imposter Syndrome is and how to tell the difference between this and feeling a natural caution or doubt. More importantly, you're going to learn how to diagnose whether you suffer from Imposter Syndrome yourself. Don't worry if you do! Imposter Syndrome is pretty normal and, thankfully, can be easily defeated, as you'll find out in the last section of this book.

Ready to enter the world of confident competence? The first step starts right here. Let's get started!

What is Imposter Syndrome?

Imposter Syndrome starts with a feeling of anxiety. It's a hint of unease that you don't know what you're doing. It's a worry you're in over your head. It's a certainty you don't know what you're doing, and everyone in the world already knows it, or if not, is about to find out. It's a sick sense of everything about to collapse around you, as though everything you've ever done is nothing more than a house of cards waiting to fall.

What's even worse is not how Imposter Syndrome is tied into your emotions, though this certainly makes it unpleasant to experience. What makes Imposter Syndrome truly nefarious is how it negates every one of your accomplishments, achievements, and honors as though they never happened.

For this reason, Imposter Syndrome is considered one of the more annoying conditions you'll experience in your life. Worse yet, the odds are fairly good you will experience it. Since Imposter Syndrome was first discovered back in 1978, it's been tracked and studied many times throughout the years. Current thought shows at least 70% of people will experience Imposter Syndrome at some point in their lifetimes, with this number climbing still higher, mostly due to the impact of social media upon our lives.

What are some of the key components of Imposter Syndrome?
Crippling self-doubt
The absolute need to do better or more than those around you
Never being able to take a compliment
Inability to see your achievements
A tendency to sabotage yourself
Constantly chasing perfection

The feeling others would do better in your job or situation
Feeling like you don't deserve what you have
Worry that someone will 'find out the truth' about you and expose you to the world as a 'fake.'

Imposter Syndrome isn't a display of healthy caution or even the normal uncertainty that might come with trying something new. It's also not a dose of modesty or even humility which is an intentional downplaying of achievement not to be seen as a braggart.

These traits can probably be better explained in the next chapter, as we explore several different types of "Imposters."

Imposter Syndrome shows up for a variety of reasons. These include:

The Past
Anytime someone pushed you to accomplish more, you likely noticed yourself having thoughts along the lines of "Wait, wasn't what I just did good enough?" If you grew up under this kind of constant pressure from the adults in your life (typically parents or other authority figures, such as teachers), you very likely internalized some feelings of not measuring up. This feeling is further underscored whenever someone has been critical of you, especially if these criticisms weren't exactly fair. The more this happened, the more likely you are to experience Imposter Syndrome as an adult.

Our Peers
Too often, our standing in a group tends to rely on our accomplishments. In other words, our social credibility relies very heavily on having more achievements, awards, or other recognition than the person next to you. This will push you harder to get ahead. While at the same time building feelings of inferiority,

especially if you're already surrounded by high achievers who always seem to outperform you at every turn.

Our 'Friends'

Not every friendship is going to be a healthy one. In some relationships, it's common to find you have a friend or two who is only there for the disaster. They're there because every time you fail, they feel better about themselves. Usually, this is the mark of someone who is immature or who has poor self-esteem themselves. Unfortunately, the damage they can do to your self-esteem can be brutal. After all, deep down, they need you to fail for them to feel good. With this in mind, they'll be quick to point out every flaw and remind you of every time where you didn't quite measure up.

Group Think

There is nothing quite so frightening as being unique. This kind of thinking generally has some pretty hardwired emotion attached to it which comes straight out of our DNA. Back in the old hunter/gatherer days, the way to stay safe was to be part of the crowd. Doing something which would separate you from the pack was generally a quick way out of the group, which is a world filled with predators was the equivalent of a death sentence. Today we still have this same fear of being alienated from the group even if we've outgrown the need for it. This is why peer pressure can be so powerful, and the idea of standing out can be terrifying. If this fear is strong in you, it can drive an absolute loathing for not fitting in, to the point where Imposter Syndrome becomes a way of life and a means of sabotaging yourself before you ever truly get started doing anything at all.

Birth Order

For whatever reason, it seems firstborn children have a slightly higher chance of suffering from Imposter Syndrome. While there isn't conclusive evidence as to why this might be so, it is thought parents put more pressure on their firstborn than on the other children in a family. Whether this is because the oldest is expected to be an example, or if it's just a matter of parents 'loosening up' as they become more relaxed with being parents, it's hard to say. Whatever the case, it has an impact on how these children grow up to think about themselves.

Parenting Style

If you grew up in the last 20 or 30 years, you likely had a more protected childhood than those of previous generations. Children who grew up in very careful environments are going to be less sure of themselves as adults. They haven't pushed themselves to 'see what they're made of' nor had they had to cope with difficult decisions or the outcomes of those decisions. When you're less sure of yourself, you're more likely to feel like an imposter than someone who has a lot of confidence built through life experience.

Genealogy
Ask any parent who has more than one child, and they'll tell you certain traits just seem to be born in a child. They will quickly identify which is their 'brave' child and which one is more timid. Some people just worry more about fitting in than others. They've always been the sort to internalize negativity. If this is true about you, you're likely to have more trouble with Imposter Syndrome. Not that this should in any way be seen as something you can't escape. You're not trapped as an imposter for your entire life. It just means you're going to have to put some more effort into learning strategies for coping with Imposter Syndrome (which we'll talk about more a bit later).

Who Suffers from Imposter Syndrome?

It might surprise you to find out just how common Imposter Syndrome is. Think about these quotes, which might surprise you when you find out who said them.

"Sometimes I wake up in the morning before going off to a shoot, and I think, I can't do this. I'm a fraud... I'm there thinking, 'Oh my God, I'm rubbish, and everyone is going to see it. They've cast the wrong person.'" – Kate Winslet

"No matter what we've done, there comes the point where you think, 'How did I get here? When are they going to discover that I am, in fact, a fraud and take everything away from me?'" – Tom Hanks

"You think, 'Why would anyone want to see me again in a movie? And I don't know how to act anyway, so why am I doing this?' "– Meryl Streep

"I have written 11 books, but each time I think, 'uh oh, they're going to find out now. I've run a game on everybody, and they're going to find me out.'" – Maya Angelou

"I have spent my years since Princeton, while at law school and in my various professional jobs, not feeling completely a part of the worlds I inhabit. I am always looking over my shoulder wondering if I measure up." – Sonia Sotomayor

These quotes come from a variety of individuals famed for their accomplishments. Think about this for a minute. Even the most successful people in the world have felt like imposters at some point or another.

This is because just about everyone has felt Imposter Syndrome at one point or another. Remember the statistic which said 70% of people had experienced this condition? This statistic came from a rigorous study, but more informal polls put this number at 87% or even higher.

It doesn't matter if you're rich or poor. Gender or sexuality doesn't come into play. Nor does education level, background, location, or any other way we like to divide people into categories. Absolutely anyone can feel like an imposter.

This alone can feel daunting. Now consider one more factor: How Imposter Syndrome holds people back.

How Imposter Syndrome Holds Us Back

Imposter Syndrome floods your brain with negative thoughts
You're more likely to procrastinate.
You take longer to get things done.
You experience a lot of uncertainty.
You don't try new things because you don't know how they'll come out.
You miss more opportunities or don't see opportunities when they come to you.
You have a harder time judging what you're capable of achieving.
You tend to set goals that are too impossible to achieve.
You miss out on time with your family as you fall into overwork patterns.
You sabotage relationships as you feel you're not worthy of your partner.
You experience burnout quicker than other people do.

Your health suffers from the added stress Imposter Syndrome creates.
You avoid networking or new relationships because you feel like you have nothing to offer.
You become an overachiever.
You experience more anxiety than those around you.
You are more likely to fail even when you do try to achieve things.
You're more prone to depression, self-harm, and suicidal thoughts.

Am I An Imposter?

Determining whether you're just feeling modest or might instead be an imposter can be a tricky thing to figure out. In this chapter, we're going to start by talking about different kinds of imposters. From there, we'll go into a series of questions that should help clarify matters a little.

The Various Types of "Imposters"

Dr. Valerie Young put considerable time into studying Imposter Syndrome for her book, "The Secret Thoughts of Professional Women." She argues that there are five very distinct types of "Imposters," which each exhibit somewhat different traits of Imposter Syndrome. As a note, don't be confused by the title of her book. While initially Imposter Syndrome was discovered when studying the problems women have in the workplace, as mentioned before, any gender can experience it. We want to take away from her book the following classifications, as she did sum up the various types of imposters quite well.

These are:
The Perfectionist
The Superman / Superwoman
The Natural Genius
The Soloist
The Expert

What you're going to find out is you're probably a blend of more than one archetype. This is part of what makes Imposter Syndrome so interesting...and so frustrating. This can make it harder to figure out just what kind of Imposter you might be. So, you might want to pay attention as you read through these descriptions and take note of anything which sounds familiar.

That said, let's dig in and get to know each of these classifications a little better.

The Perfectionist

No one can ever set the bar quite so high as the perfectionist. Now some might argue this is a good thing. Aren't perfectionists good at doing things well? Well, not as much as you might think. They want to do things well, but they'll take a long time to get tasks done because things will never be quite good enough or will need to be tweaked again. And again. And again.

Their problem has to do with being in control of the outcome, making them terrible procrastinators and micromanagers when you put them in charge. This all takes on a nasty turn, though, when you examine them in the light of Imposter Syndrome.

The Perfectionist is never going to get anything "right" to the extent they want it, and as a result, will beat themselves up endlessly for not achieving the goal in the way they want to. They see themselves as a failure, even when they've already succeeded past what's expected of them and will continue to see themselves as failure should they surpass even those levels of excellence.

The Superman/Superwoman

Need something done? Now here's your personality type who's ready to take on anything no matter how busy they are. This individual is the overachiever. They put in more time than anyone when they're at work, to the point where it's a wonder if they ever go home. If they do, you can bet they're still working on the weekend. To Superman or Superwoman, there is no such thing as a day off. Nor do they limit their projects to just one area in life. These guys would put a juggler to shame for how skillfully they'll keep all the balls in the air (so to speak). Their work-life, home life, and even how they parent their kids are all about quantity at all costs.

Why do they work themselves to the bone, giving up so much of themselves to do it?

At the heart of the Superman or Superwoman is the person who's so convinced they have no true worth that they need constant validation from those around them. They live for the praise which others heap on them, even while disbelieving every word of it. Not that this stops them from going out and doing it all over again. The sad thing is, while this person might accomplish crazy amounts of work in a day, they can never truly enjoy the outcome. Imposter syndrome tells them there's still more needing to get done.

The Natural Genius

The moment you see the word "genius," you probably picture someone like Newton or Einstein. Super smart people who are very high achievers. While this might be true to an extent, the natural genius is a bit different. At the same time, this individual is very, very good in some areas of life but isn't necessarily out of the ordinary in other regards. The natural genius typically has an innate talent in one very specific area.

Think about it this way. Some people might be natural geniuses when it comes to math. They just have a knack for understanding numbers and probably did fairly well in school...until it came time to show their work.

This is the problem with natural genius. They might understand things almost instinctively, but they're not necessarily good at explaining how they got their answers. This also means the natural genius is very often frustrated when they come up against knowledge they must work to learn. More often than not, they truly don't understand how to learn what they don't have, at least not on the first try. This is where Imposter Syndrome kicks in. To someone who knows everything about a subject, this frustration makes them feel they've failed. They might even fight against learning, getting caught up in self-doubt until they hit a shame cycle and spiral on down.

Why? Because they're so used to knowledge, this comes easy. They can't handle it when their genius betrays them, and they find out they're not as infallible as they might have thought. It's as though this single failure negates everything else they've accomplished.

The Soloist

If you've ever felt like the last thing you wanted was for others to find out you didn't know what you were doing, you already understand the soloist. This individual is the lone wolf. They'll do everything on their own, precisely because they feel like such an imposter.

For this reason, soloists are sometimes seen as antisocial, though this might not be the case at all. Their desire to push people away stems entirely from fear of being found out, so deep down, they might truly want help or to at least have the support of others.

But if they're flying solo for too long, this could eventually change. The hardcore soloist might start to resent the fact they can never get help on things and even hate how others seem to have no problem at all with having help when they must do everything alone.

The Expert

"I just need one more thing" might well be the mantra of The Expert. No matter what they're doing or how familiar they might be with the process they need, they're still going to feel like they don't have the knowledge or skills to get things done. These are the people who want to go back for a little more research. They're constantly double and triple-checking themselves or are looking for additional training.

This isn't to say everyone who likes research is an 'expert.' Remember, the root of this particular imposter is the feeling they have of not being qualified or capable. We all feel this way sometimes, especially when we're doing something new. But if you're burying yourself in certifications, college courses, and other material but still never feel ready or even remotely prepared, you're likely an Expert. Especially if you find this need to learn more is keeping you from starting what needs to get done.

This list does not encompass every kind of imposter, though it is a good jumping-off point for understanding them. Remember, any time you find yourself second-guessing yourself, feeling like you're unqualified, or otherwise become panicky at the thought of someone just gave you praise or a promotion, you might well be slipping into imposter syndrome.

Every variety you see here has one crucial thing in common: the imposter never feels like they belong where they are or deserve the praise they receive,

Imposter Syndrome Self-Test

By now, you might be wondering if you might well be an imposter yourself. If this is the case, consider these questions carefully:

The Perfectionist
Do you frequently feel like you don't have enough time to complete things even though others get the same tasks done in less time?
Do you feel like things will never be 'good enough'?
Do you go back to tweak things to the point where it's difficult to declare a project 'finished'?
Do you have trouble accepting a compliment?
Do you frequently think they've picked the wrong person when someone wants to give you recognition for something you've done?
Do you have a sense of 'having gotten away with something when you turn in work, and people accept it as being okay?

Do you feel like things are never done?
Have people called you a perfectionist?

The Superman / Superwoman
Are you known for getting things done?
Do you frequently take on new tasks even though you're already busy?
Do you accomplish more than those around you and still feel like it's not enough?
Do you keep working long after everyone else has gone home for the day?
Do you keep so busy your family is starting to wonder where you are?
Do you work many extra hours, evenings, and weekends even when financially you don't need to?
Are you secretly proud of how much work you get done?
Even if you're secretly proud of how much work you're getting done, do you still feel like you could do better and do still more?
Have you been accused of being an overachiever?

Do you frequently have many projects going on at once?
Do you tend to start a lot of things but have trouble finishing them?

The Natural Genius
Do some things come very easily to you?
Do you become frustrated when you don't understand something immediately?
Do you struggle with learning new things even though you're knowledgeable in other areas?
Are you considered an expert in some areas but have trouble explaining your knowledge?
Do you feel like a failure if you don't understand something immediately?
Do you obsess about what you don't know when you know many other things?
Do you feel stupid when something needs to be explained to you?
Are you sure everyone else sees you as stupid if you don't understand something?

The Soloist

Do you frequently feel like you're pretending to be something you're not?

Do you deliberately choose projects where you can work alone?

Do you micromanage things?

Have people said you're not a team player?

Do you push people away, so they don't find out about the 'real' you?

When doing group projects, do you volunteer to take on a piece by yourself, so you don't have to work with others?

The Expert

Do you constantly seek out certifications, degrees, or other achievements as a means of showing others you do know things?

Do you still feel like you don't know enough despite this?

Do you get stuck in research to the point where it's hard to begin the project itself?

Are you constantly fact-checking things you already know because you don't trust yourself?

Do you feel like you shouldn't apply for a job unless you have every qualification they might need?
Do you panic at the idea of being hired in a position you're not trained to do?
Have you ever been surprised by a promotion because you don't feel like you deserve it? Has this happened more than once?
Do you feel like you got lucky if you were promoted or received some sort of commendation?
Do you put down your achievements, telling yourself anyone could do what you do?
Do you insist your accomplishments are because of people around you rather than anything you gained through your own merits?

General Questions
Do you feel like you got where you are today only because of connections or other people giving you a hand up?
Do you think people praise you only because they're being polite or must for some reason?

Do you tell people you faked it when you do receive praise?

Do you think you faked it and somehow accomplished what you did?

Do you minimize your input, as though you're not sure of what you're saying even though you are?

Do you feel like other people have it easier than you?

Do you frequently look for validation from others?

Does the idea of success scare you?

A few things to note: Everyone will experience some of these symptoms at some point in their life. What you're looking for is a pattern or a frequency of "yes" answers.

Second, and more importantly, if you do wind up saying "yes" to many of these, there's absolutely no reason to panic. Suffering from Imposter Syndrome does not make you a bad person, and no, you're NOT a failure. This just happens to be where you are right now. There is help. The next chapter has some great tips designed to get you back on track in no time!

Dealing with Imposter Syndrome

If you're someone who experiences Imposter Syndrome, this chapter is for you. Here is where you're going to find several techniques to help you deal with Imposter Syndrome, so you can reclaim your life and enjoy every success to the fullest. Even more exciting is the last section, which tells you how to keep Imposter Syndrome away for good. Think about it: No more living life feeling like a failure!

Techniques for Dealing with Imposter Syndrome

The trick to dealing with Imposter Syndrome is building an awareness of your thoughts, followed by actions to rewire those thoughts. Sometimes these tips are going to use distraction to keep you from feeling this way.

Other times you'll find you're simply using a different script when it comes to dealing with the voice in your head. None of these tips are meant to be permanent fixes but are intended to keep Imposter Syndrome from ruling your life.

Remind Yourself Everyone is an Imposter
Remember those earlier statistics? Just about everyone feels this way sometimes. It's normal. Don't let your Imposter Syndrome become one more way you beat yourself up.

Name the Imposter Bothering You
Sometimes it helps to distance yourself from the thoughts of being an imposter by recognizing the imposter you're dealing with at the moment. Say, "Oh, that's the soloist trying to get me alone." Or, for added fun, give it a name you can call it. "Well, it looks like Myrtle the Mutterer is back to tell me I'm an idiot." Remember, if you can laugh at the Imposter, it no longer holds power over you.

Honestly Assess Your Abilities
When you feel like an imposter, you start thinking you're not good at anything. This is a lie. Everyone is good at something. Start keeping a list of your best talents. Add to it as you discover more. Re-read it when you need a boost.

Admit to Accomplishment
Imposters have a hard time seeing any success at all. When you finish something, start recognizing this as an accomplishment to break this cycle. Say it out loud. There's nothing wrong with sharing the news!

Celebrate Every Success
Every time you finish a project or do something well, call attention to it. Reward yourself with something small or set up a brag board for your eyes only to remind yourself of just how many things you get right.

Act Quickly
Imposter Syndrome is great at making you procrastinate about doing things by telling yourself you're not ready. If you've already been preparing for a while, tell yourself today is the day to dive in. Act quickly before you can talk yourself out of it.

Avoid Validation
Most people with Imposter Syndrome tend to look to those around them for reassurance they're doing things right. The problem? They don't always give it. Stop looking for validation from others. Instead, start a practice of validating yourself.

Embrace Criticism
Okay, maybe you're not the best at some things. But instead of listening to your imposter making a list of your faults, why not seek out some constructive criticism from someone you trust? They're apt to be way more honest and a whole lot kinder than you'll ever be. You'll also

know where you truly do need to make improvements...and, more importantly, where you don't.

Look for Small Areas of Improvement

If you've gotten some constructive criticism and want to act on it, don't fall into the all-or-nothing mindset of the imposter. Instead, take these areas of needed improvement in small stages. You'll feel a lot better about yourself if you start slow and won't burn out as quickly.

Ask for Help

Imposter Syndrome tries to hide when you're floundering. This only makes you sink all the faster. Instead of suffering in silence, trying desperately to keep the secret of your uncertainty, why not ask for help instead?

Accept Assistance

Asking for help is never enough. You still need to accept assistance when it's offered. This might be a good idea to get in the habit of doing, even when you haven't asked for help. Haven't you heard the old saying, "Many hands make light work"?

Learn What You Need, When You Need it
Don't get caught up in doing additional research you don't need or pursuing added education and certifications which have nothing to do with what you're currently doing. Both of these things are signs of imposter syndrome out of control. Instead, focus more on the here and now. What do you need to learn at this moment? What will you need next? Let the distant future worry about itself for a while.

Ask Questions
Imposters rarely ask for clarification because they're afraid others will notice their ignorance. Instead of worrying about what others think, wouldn't it be better to get the information you need when you need it?

Find Support
Studies have shown people who tell a trusted friend or mentor about feeling like an imposter are more likely to feel better much more quickly than someone suffering through imposter syndrome on their own. Find someone you can be honest with about what you're going through.

Mentor
If you don't feel particularly strong in an area where others think of you as an expert, consider teaching others what you do know. You'll probably be pleasantly surprised by just how knowledgeable you are. Also, teaching is a great way to firm up your confidence in your skillset.

Enjoy Imperfection
So, you're not perfect. Does it matter? To the Imposter, it does. To the rest of the world, not so much. Also, did you know that in some

cultures, flawed things are considered the most beautiful?

Allow Others to See the Flaws
Speaking of flaws, how about letting others see your own instead of putting so much effort into hiding them? Why not share your rough draft? Send out the proposal, which isn't perfect. There's nothing wrong with letting others see work in progress sometimes.

Cull Out Comparisons
You're never going to feel good about yourself or what you're capable of if you're constantly comparing yourself to those around you. There will always be someone better at something than you are. This is a simple truth in life. There is nothing to be gained by dwelling on this.

Refocus Energies
Imposter Syndrome needs to be fed to survive. Instead of getting caught up where you're going wrong, shift your attention to something else

for a while? Ask yourself how you can help someone else instead right now.

Learn How to Deal with Compliments
When someone says something nice about you, what do you do? Instead of avoiding taking credit for doing something right or negating the accomplishment, practice saying "Thank you." Then take note of the compliment. Write it down so you can read it over again later. Compliments are worth keeping!

Do Something
Imposter Syndrome can stall you out. Either you get caught up procrastinating because you don't think you can do the task correctly, or you don't even begin because you're sure it's going to fail. When this happens, find an activity you can do. ANY action is better than no action at all. Even if you don't immediately dive in on what you've been procrastinating about, you will discover it's easier to dig into work later if you've been doing something else for a while.

Fake It
The Imposter might tell you you're faking it. Well, maybe you are. Ask yourself if that's necessarily a bad thing? Sometimes we all need to fake a little confidence or push on as though we know what we're doing. If it's working, there's no reason to stop or feel bad about it.

Know You're Not All That
Okay, sometimes we all need a humanity check. If you're caught up in the perfection thing or are overachieving to the point of driving you (and everyone else) crazy, you might want to remind yourself you're not God. No one can do it all. Why are you trying to?

Expect Mistakes
Don't allow your inner imposter to internalize mistakes and use them against you. Nothing is ever going to go right 100% of the time. Tell yourself mistakes are inevitable. When they do

happen, remember it's normal and part of the process.

Consider Your Mortality

This seems kind of grim, but we're all going to die someday. Do you want to spend your days on earth feeling like an imposter? Sometimes it helps to focus on the big picture by visualizing instead how you want to live your life and how you want to be remembered someday.

Own Your Success

You have every right to take pride in your accomplishments. Instead of explaining away when you do succeed, take a deep breath and allow yourself to feel the joy of knowing you did well.

Know Your Value

Hey, you're an incredible person. Why are you listening to someone telling you you're not? Make a list of all your best qualities. If you're having trouble doing this, ask someone else to help you make your list. Read over it often, whenever you need a boost.

Talk to Someone
If you've tried everything else and are still floundering, it might be you need a little help to get started. There's nothing wrong with seeking professional help when you need it. Seeking out a counselor or a licensed psychologist might be the boost you need to get back on track.

Keeping Imposter Syndrome Away for Good

In this section, you're going to find several steps designed to attack the roots of Imposter Syndrome. You're going to explore why you feel the way you do and explore methods that will dig down to shift your thinking entirely.

Recognize What's Going On
This should almost go without saying, but sometimes we don't always recognize where we are internally until we're already neck-deep into the negative emotions. With this in mind, part of your plan to keep Imposter Syndrome away is to spot the signs when you feel it coming on. The moment you feel those old thought patterns wrapping around you, stop and ask yourself if this might be Imposter Syndrome.

Perform a Reality Check
If it is Imposter Syndrome, it's crucial to ask yourself what you're reacting to. What are you feeling uncertain about? Is there any basis for feeling this way?

Accept the Insecurity
If there is a basis for these thoughts, it's important to validate this. So, if you're feeling a little lost because you're in a new place, remind yourself this is a perfectly normal feeling. People will feel lost when they're someplace new. This doesn't make you an imposter.

Negate the Nonsensical
If there is no basis for the thought, it's time to remind yourself that while your emotions are valid and you might be feeling things that make you uncertain, there is no reason to feel this way. List how this line of thinking can be considered false. For example, if you feel like you don't know enough to perform a certain task, but you've done this task before, you'll

want to remind yourself in detail of how well you've performed this task in the past.

Adjust the Thought Processes
Usually, when you're falling into these patterns again, you'll note some negative thoughts in the background, which are not only setting you up for Imposter Syndrome but are inflating these emotions. Put the brakes on this kind of internal dialogue and instead focus on the most positive thought you can use to replace it.

Move Past Mistakes
If these thoughts are cropping up because of failure, you're going to want to have a script ready for what to tell yourself. Include a reminder that everyone makes mistakes and instructions on how to look for what can be learned from the experience instead of falling into a cycle of negativity and self-blame.

What About the Rules?

It might be you're still battling Imposter Syndrome because of something someone else said to you a long time ago, which has now become a rule for your life. Consider whether what you're feeling might be one of those 'unbreakable' laws which were never of your own making, such as "You must always finish what you've started" or "You must have things perfect before you turn them in." Now ask yourself if this is a rule you want to live by? Are there better rules you could create and apply to your life instead? Things like, "It's okay to walk away from a project which no longer brings pleasure or satisfaction" or "Sometimes it's okay for things to be just 'good enough' rather than perfect."

Picture A New Outcome
Forget the disaster movie trying to play in your head. Think about the situation which has triggered the feelings of being an imposter. Now picture the outcome you're like to have instead. Imagine what success looks like and the steps you took to get there.

Reward Right Behavior
As you step back away from feelings of being an Imposter, give yourself praise. Never, under ANY circumstances, do you want to beat yourself up for having these feelings or for not reacting fast enough. Instead, celebrate catching yourself and doing a great job in squelching these feelings before they got very far. Great job, you're doing amazing!

Wrap up

Are you feeling a little more confident? Hopefully, by now, you are. If not, don't give up hope. Keep working on the steps in the last chapter, and you'll get there. It's a matter of being patient with yourself. More importantly, you need to be consistent. In time, these new thought processes will become a habit, and from there, a way of life.

It's a wonderful feeling knowing you're worthy of every success. When you reach this point, you'll know you're legit. Even better? The rest of the world will know it too.

So, hang in there! You're not an imposter, nor will you ever need to feel like one again. The new you starts today, with a new way of looking at the world. How exciting to finally see yourself as you truly are!

Eliminating Self Defeating Behaviors

No doubt, you have heard of the expression "getting in your own way". It seems like one of those expressions that's been around forever, but it can be attributed to professional baseball player Steve Carlton, who said "You've gotta find a way to get out of your own way, so you can progress in life."

It's a quote that nicely sums up one of modern society's biggest issues – that of self-defeating behavior.

"Author of his own misfortune" and "architect of his own demise" are further examples of expressions based on quotes by the Roman statesman Appius Claudius from 300 BC. More accurately, Claudius said, "Each man is the smith of his own fortune" and "each man is the architect of his own fate" but the message is clear – we have a choice to embrace positive behavior and reap its rewards, or to allow ourselves fall victim to self-defeating behaviors by literally, getting in our own way.

It's easy to watch a TV program or movie and see quite plainly how the characters onscreen engage in behavior that does nothing but bring them pain and tragedy. In fact, often it seems like the more tragedy, the more popular the show.

Books, too, are a great source for stories of self-sabotage. William Shakespeare was perhaps the master of telling stories that involved characters whose lives were made miserable, or were even ended, by their own self sabotaging behavior. So no, there's no blaming technology for this one.

What's not so easy is to see how or why we behave in ways that do nothing but bring us pain and suffering yet continue to do so despite the fact.

Where does the blame for such behavior lie? By the time you finish reading this report you may have a different answer to that question than you do now.

What Self-Defeating Habits Are

A self-defeating behavior is not necessarily one that's full of all the drama that you might expect. Self-sabotage is not limited to extreme acts such as hardcore drug abuse or alcoholism. Instead, it's a behavior that distracts you from your goals in life or leaves you feeling tired or ashamed. In other words, sometimes we behave in a way that we know will have a negative result for us but continue to behave in that manner anyway. Often, it's with the expectation that by undergoing some harmful result now, we put off a more harmful result later.

As author Anais Nin said, "We don't see things as they are, we see them as we are."

Common Self-Defeating Behaviors

Examples of self-defeating behavior make for a long list, but the following should give you some idea of how people indulge in them:

Not taking our goals seriously. We fail to take our goals seriously when we mismanage and waste our time. A common way we do this is to create To Do lists and then ignore them.

Spending an inappropriate amount of time on helping others achieve their goals rather than on meeting our own.

Giving in to our children's demands for the sake of temporary respite from an unpleasant situation, like when they are screaming or crying.

Deciding to diet or cut down on alcohol then going for a burger or a beer as soon as the opportunity to do so presents itself.

Spending money on fad purchases when our bank account is in overdraft.

Wanting to spend more time with our kids but then telling ourselves we are too tired.

Procrastinating when we know our livelihood depends on us taking action.

Caring too much about what others think of us and adapting our behavior to compensate.

Not taking chances, such as on a new hobby or relationship because we fear failure.

Not working on a new project because we fear success.

Expecting perfectionism from both ourselves and other people.

Taking criticism personally and reacting in ways that are out of proportion to the criticism.

Expecting to get by without helping others or asking others for help.

Not getting enough sleep, especially when we know we have a difficult day ahead or an important meeting in the morning.

Staying in relationships that we know are wrong for us.

There are many different ways each of these behaviors manifest themselves. Each one may impact us differently than they impact other people.

Just why we behave in ways that serve to sabotage our own success has been the subject of great debate. Freud hypothesized that we subconsciously have a death wish, and that explains away our behavior. Except it's not really that simple. It's also a little over dramatic.

There are three commonly accepted types of self-sabotage.
The first is the type of self-harm that is intentional, such as those who cut themselves or engage in masochistic practices.

The second is called "tradeoff" and involves making the choice to do something that has an inherent risk of possible negative consequences. Smokers fit this model, as every cigarette is literally a tradeoff between the illusory enjoyment gained by feeding the drug addiction and the possibility of incurring life-threatening diseases.

The third type involves counterproductive strategies, by which the self-saboteur is unaware that their actions will have a negative result. Such strategies form behaviors that are less evident as being harmful than the others

because we don't always see them for what they are. It can take an accumulation of these experiences before we truly start to understand that there is a problem.
The reasons behind all three behaviors are similar: a lack of emotional self-management.

Self-control or self-discipline is usually an issue for those whose behavior impedes their personal actualization.

Behaving in ways that do harm to our self-esteem, or our physical or financial wellbeing may seem paradoxical. After all, why would anyone do such things? Don't we all strive for success in our lives? Wouldn't it make sense to concentrate our efforts purely on self-betterment? After all, wouldn't the results of self-betterment - the financial security, the home comforts, the social life and love life that nourishes us - be just a dream come true!

But life isn't black and white. Often, we view events as trade-offs against others. We accept one setback rather than risk a greater one. Like golfers, we seem to operate a handicap system in life, and as only the best golfers understand, getting good at the game involves a lot of work on yourself.

Guilt and blame are central to self-defeat - often waiting until success is just in sight before making an appearance to ask us just who the hell we think we are to attain it.

Guilt

Those who suffer from self-defeat usually have difficulty internalizing their own success. They don't feel deserving of it, which makes them feel guilty for achieving it with no apparent struggle. They don't believe success can be that easy. And it happens regardless of the fact they may have spent years trying to succeed. Ironically, they may have wasted those years because they couldn't comprehend how well equipped they were to succeed.

Others' expectations of us can create guilt, such as for those who enter into a profession that goes against that which their parents or spouses wanted them to enter.

Guilty too, the people who rise to fame or fortune based on their looks, family connections, or a career that is commonly viewed as "easy" or at least unworthy of the high salaries they command, such as acting or playing football.

Creating a handicap to account for possible failure may take the blame from your shoulders for a brief period, but it does little to manage the feelings of guilt.

Guilt rears its ugly head again in another behavior tactic designed to manage expectations: excuse making. Self-defeatists tend toward using excuses to mask behaviors such as procrastination and other situations where their personal accountability comes into question. The guilt of the initial behavior is compounded by the excuses and forces the self-saboteur into proving the excuse to be real in their own minds, which carries fresh guilt with it.

These kinds of excuses are referred to as pathological excuses because they tend to exaggerate facts. It soon becomes that the excuse maker believes his own excuses and so it becomes a cycle.

Cycles and patterns are often seen in self-defeatist behaviors as we will come to see.

Blame

Believe it or not, you really can blame your parents for this bad habit. Indirectly. And only if you're say, 5 years of age.

When we are kids, we tend to point our finger elsewhere to escape parental anger. We hate to disappoint them, so we tell them someone else did the bad thing. It's handy to have someone else to take the blame. (Ever notice how often those people weren't around at the time?)

As we mature, we start to take responsibility for our actions. Mostly. Whether you blame others, or blame yourself, it's the kind of negative behavior that will ultimately lead you back to guilt or harm you in other ways.

Blame often points to a hidden insecurity in someone's personality and there are a few different motivations that may be at work:

Controlling someone else
The blamer uses their victim's emotional reaction to instill them with guilt, fear or insecurity.

Feeling controlled by someone else, or loss of control

The blamer dislikes the situation they are being placed in and point the finger as an escape from unpleasantness. Often, the self-defeatist proclaims that if it weren't for the demands placed on them by their kids/spouse/parent, they'd have the time and energy to succeed.

Truly successful people will make that time by getting up earlier, staying up later, getting fitter to cope with the extra demands. The self-defeatist points to others and blames them for their lack of progress.

When they do this, they are giving themselves an imaginary handicap to allow them to maintain some semblance of self-esteem. For so long as they can push the blame onto someone else's shoulders they'll feel okay about their own self-imposed limitations.

Emulating parental influence
Sadly, some parents never became aware enough to take responsibility for their own actions. They argue with each other again and again, never realizing that they are teaching the blame game to their own kids. And with that lack of self-knowledge comes the inability to teach their kids how to become the kind of adults who take responsibility for their own actions.

Similarly, if a child were to be punished even though their behavior was good, or rewarded despite bad behavior, it instils the message that their behavior doesn't matter. This seeming lack of control can cause a learned helplessness.

Inability to accept circumstances for what they are
Sadly, some people undergo severe emotional reactions to situations in their lives. It could happen to any of us - particularly if we invest a lot of our identity in our relationships with

other people or anything we view as being core to our social status or wellbeing. It only needs that person or status symbol to be taken away in order for our world view to change drastically.

We see examples of this around us all the time when we see high profile marriages fall apart. When one partner invests so much of their identity in being part of a relationship with the other, it can be devastating when it ends. They literally feel like they are losing part of themselves. It's true of course, because they made part of themselves depend on the other person's availability instead of nurturing themselves.

Insecurity
Some people just need to affirm that they are the ones who are morally or intellectually superior. Blaming others affirms their position in society. This kind of blamer is probably the most irritating to other people and the most

avoided in social situations. They usually carry the personality traits of continuously interrupting others to assert their view and sometimes actually changing their story to maintain the position of blame on someone else.

Self-blame leads to a guilt cycle that's hard to get out of: you blame yourself so you feel guilty, then the guilt ensures you feel responsible and deserve blame, and so the pattern continues.

Blaming others doesn't measure up too well either. It's a classic avoidance behavior to avoid the consequences of our actions and those actions can be big and scary. Losing a loved one or going to jail are extreme examples.

People also tend to avoid contact with people who like to blame others for their own shortfalls. They are hard work to be around, and a few hours spent with one can feel like an exhausting day. You may notice that a lot of people who exhibit self-defeating behaviors eventually isolate themselves to the point where they are asking 'why do I have no friends and why does no one seems to like me?'.

Having Unreasonable Expectations
Managing our expectations is a factor that contributes to self-defeat, but not in the manner you may expect. While we're often told to manage our expectations, i.e. not expect too much in case we are disappointed, it's not usually clear that if we expect to perform a given task poorly, we are more likely to perform it poorly. If we had approached the task with a degree of confidence we would have had far greater success, but by internalizing the expectation that we do poorly we merely establish behavior that follows suit.

Shiny Object Syndrome
As the world evolves, and with it the sheer number of possibilities that open up to us begin to overwhelm, the mental sickness of the 21st

century has become Shiny Object Syndrome. It describes the act of buying into every new idea that comes your way in an effort to achieve some kind of success, somewhere.

It will often mean the sufferer spends money on some kind of training course or accessory that will help them become better at their intended venture: writing, playing an instrument, a new sport or hobby.

Before they even get to grips with it, something else comes along and captures their attention and then they are off chasing that new shiny object in the same way crows are attracted to shiny objects.

People who suffer from this syndrome never gain any pleasure from their purchases and never achieve success with them because they are too busy buying the next shiny thing to come along.

How Self-Defeating Behaviors are formed

Self-defeating behaviors are formed when bad habits stack up. They don't just appear overnight.

Usually, they are formed when we experience an extremely emotional situation, and often it's our reaction to that situation that lays the foundation for the habit and subsequent behavior.

This means that you may have built up such a variety of bad habits that you have quite a few self-defeating behaviors that have come about as a result.

When an emotional upheaval occurs, it tends to hardwire our reaction to it into our self-learning process, which is what makes recognizing this type of behavior so difficult. The next time we experience the same emotion, or something similar to it, we react in the same way, building a cycle or pattern of behavior.

For example, Jane meets a guy who she falls head over heels in love with when she is in her late teens. Around the same time, there's a song that plays on the radio quite often and it reminds her of him. She loves the cologne he wears, and she associates it with him. And she comes to admire musicians for their talent, because he is one.

The relationship ends badly, and pretty soon Jane hates that song, avoids anyone who wears that cologne and insists she'll never date a musician again.

She has now formed habits that mean she's cut herself off from a variety of different men in her life.

Avoidance becomes habitual: avoidance of pain, fear, loss and any other strong emotions.

In this example, it may seem like no big deal that Jane doesn't date musicians, but patterns of behavior tend to include generalization of events.

Jane was hurt by a musician, so all musicians will hurt her. What happens if she went to a dentist who made some unfortunate error in the care of her teeth? Would she then decide that all dentists are incompetent and never visit one again?

If the reaction to the initial emotional trauma is avoidance, and so is the next reaction (because that's what we've learned from last time) then it's not long before that reaction is habitual – and therefore a behavior pattern.

Each time we give in to self-defeating behavior we compound the effect of the habit. Einstein said that the definition of insanity was to continue to repeat the same actions, expecting a different outcome, and in some way we are guilty of this.

It's only when the reaction is handled responsibly that we avoid or break the habits that build over time.

Causes of current self-sabotage include:

The Past
An inability to learn from past mistakes – or let go of past events – tends to form behaviors that do little to serve you today.

Self-Identity
When self-defeat becomes a habitual activity, it becomes so ingrained in your psyche that it's really difficult to recognize. You'll even hear people who say things like "I knew it was too

good to be true," or "This kind of thing is always happening to me."

They come to believe that they just can't achieve their goals because something ingrained in their genetic makeup won't allow them.

Such individuals' language is peppered with statements like "I'm such a loser," and "No one could love someone like me."

Attention Seeking
Self-defeatists often have an inability to function well in social situations. They tend to play on sympathy from others as a means to get the attention they crave (and they often crave it due to the isolation their behaviors incur). When they get the attention they want, it solidifies the habit because their experience is that by playing the "poor me" card they get attention, so they continue to do so over and over again.

Always Making Excuses

When self-defeat has become a firm habit, the victim will seek refuge in excuses. He will tend to make excuses for missing deadlines, not completing work, and anything else he can get away with. In this way, excuses are similar to blame – he is merely shifting the blame from himself.

Excuses are dangerous because the one making the excuse tends to start believing their own excuses. They see a pattern of interruptions and roadblocks that simply don't exist in reality. Yet they begin to believe they do, just by repeatedly using them as excuses. Like many other self-defeating behaviors, excuses become a self-fulfilling prophecy.

Procrastination

There is scientific data that shows procrastination to be a feature of our biological makeup that evolved to keep us safe. Basically, our amygdala (lizard brain) confuses the stress of a deadline with a fight or flight situation. The resulting overwhelm causes us to freeze.

That paralyzing sensation is probably how rabbits feel when caught in headlights.

The upside of this seeming weak link that Mother Nature inflicted on us (and much like almost all self-destructive behavior) is that it's curable once we are aware of the nature of the beast.

Learned Helplessness

When faced with the responsibility of making choices, the self-defeatist may disassociate themselves from the situation entirely. Refusing to face responsibility means never having to make the wrong choice – and hence it's another example of (say it along with me) avoidance.

An example of learned helplessness would be someone whose bank account is in constant overdraft. Whenever the bank sends a statement, they avoid opening it and face the responsibility. Instead, the letter goes unopened into the back of a drawer, destined eventually for the bin.

Next time the credit card bill arrives, they continue with the same behavior, and then pretty soon it's with the mortgage account.

This person has told themselves that they can't deal with finances; they just don't understand all that stuff. Then their behavior pattern has helped them learn to become helpless in situations that involve some kind of financial responsibility.

Stopping Short of Success

The really soul-destroying aspect of self-sabotage is that it often happens with success in sight. Many self-defeatists who have become aware enough to recognize their problem will tell you that it's usually when success in a venture is almost inevitable that they stop and switch focus to something else.

They have become so comfortable with failure that they can't move beyond it. They can't internalize success as a concept that applies to them.

Perhaps you know someone who finishes plotting a book only to go and start a new one or start a business doing one thing only to change track as soon as it's almost ready to make money.

Success is such a foreign concept that it brings with it the fear of the unknown – and the learned reaction to fear is to avoid the cause of it.

Perfectionism

The idea that we can do everything ourselves and do it perfectly is a false one. Many people suffer great disappointment at the realization that their efforts will never yield the type of results they expect of themselves. They then find it easier to keep putting off taking any kind of action because the settings for their success are never just right.

They want to become a singer, but they don't have the right microphone to use when they sing at their first gig. They don't have the right word processor, so they never get around to writing that book they have inside them. It's always too late or too early to start something, or the perfect materials aren't available.

Effects of Self-Destructive Behaviors
Self-defeating behaviors are everywhere around us, so it might seem that it's perfectly okay to have a few. It may seem as if everyone has them, so what's the harm? Surely they are just quaint little idiosyncrasies that make up who we are.

But they're just like puppies. Eventually they turn into big, hairy dogs that go to the toilet on your carpet if you don't train them right.

Typically, sufferers will experience:

Isolation
Poor career results
Low self esteem
Relationship difficulties
Addiction

Isolation
As we have seen throughout our examination of self-saboteurs' behavior patterns, their poor

emotional management tends to push them towards feelings and situations of isolation.

Isolation on its own can be unpleasant, but it's just the beginning of a worsening situation. "No man is an island" became a cliché for a reason. We rely on others in our community to provide us with friendship, understanding, supplies, financial support, employment, security and assistance.

Human beings are social creatures. We can't do everything, so we depend on others to be strong where we are weak. Perfectionism is when we think we can do everything ourselves and it makes our results intermittent and weak.

Career
Every career requires of its employee that they be willing and able to work within a team. That's not going to work if you are
busy blaming others for their failures
being a poor timekeeper

jumping projects before they are seen through to completion

are so easily offended you prefer to sit alone in the canteen rather than with your colleagues

Low Self Esteem

- It might seem obvious, but isolation from your peers and persistent failure to achieve your goals will have a detrimental effect on your self-esteem.

- Low self-esteem in itself is an issue that causes self-perpetuating misery through behavior that the sufferer would otherwise not engage in, such as downplaying or ignoring their positive qualities,
- self-criticism
- feel inferior to others
- use negative language to describe themselves

- engage in negative self-talk
- self-blame
- disbelieve positive comments made by others about themselves

While self-defeating behavior causes low self-esteem, the low self-esteem brings with it a whole slew of its own issues such as:
- Depression and sadness from the sufferer's constant negative self-talk
- Fear of failure from self-doubt
- Avoiding new responsibility for fear of judgement if they fail
- Relationship problems that they might otherwise walk away from but don't because they feel they should be happy with what they can get as they are so unlovable.
- Self-abuse or simply a learned inability to look after themselves in basic ways such as brushing their teeth, shaving or washing their clothes frequently.

- Self-abuse in terms of alcohol abuse and addictive behaviors like smoking or other drug abuse.

All the problems listed above can become serious long-term issues if allowed to continue unaddressed.

Chasing Satisfaction Outside of Yourself

Most successful people gain some kind of intrinsic satisfaction from what they do. They enjoy the process of striving for their goals. They enjoy writing their music, playing their sport, or even examining their company's blue widgets for defects. They develop real skill in what they do. It's for this reason that there exist people who get paid $500 for washing celebrities' cars.

But when you start to chase notoriety or money for its own sake, you become enslaved to working for satisfaction from outside of yourself. That doesn't ever satisfy in the same way as the inner satisfaction of really enjoying what you do.

How to Eliminate Self-Defeating Behaviors

It might seem like a line from a Disney movie, but just becoming aware of the chinks in your armor is enough to start making the kind of changes you need to make if you want to stop sabotaging your own success and start achieving the life you truly want.

Here's a quick exercise to help you:

If you were to imagine yourself in the future right now, how would you expect yourself to feel if you were to be truly happy?

Now ask yourself, as Future You, what you need to change about your past self in order to get where you are now?

Spend some time on this exercise and don't be tempted to skip it. The answers won't be immediately obvious, but with a little introspection you will find some of your negative behaviors.

You might say, I want more money in the bank, I want to be in a relationship that makes me feel positive and good about myself, or you might say, I want to achieve a pay increase at work.

Whatever your decision is, it will start to narrow down the behaviors that are preventing you from achieving that goal in the present. Hindsight is always 20/20, so looking back at present you as if you are looking at yourself in the past makes your viewpoint much less biased.

It's also worth remembering that your present actions determine your future self, so a moment's reflection on your thought process every time you feel a negative emotion may be all it takes to start unearthing the hidden causes.

No matter what your agenda is, once you make the decision to quit sabotaging your own success, it's time to start taking action.

Negative Self Talk

One method of eliminating negative self-talk that's been suggested by experts is to imagine that everything that goes on in our heads as if it were being broadcast on the screen above a major league baseball game. Would you feel proud of what's going on in your head, or would you be embarrassed by it?

Chances are, there will be quite a lot of thoughts you wouldn't feel too proud of if they became public knowledge. Sometimes when we talk negatively to ourselves it has a habit of becoming generally negative and can go on to include how we talk to ourselves about other people, too.

Most negative self-talk lacks any firm foundation in fact - it's merely an emotion that is being allowed to run free without supervision.

Negative Comparisons to Others

Everyone is different - and everyone appeals to different types of people. When a well-known brand launches a new product - say a new brand of Coke, or a different type of vacuum cleaner, the company behind the brand doesn't try to appeal to everyone. Instead, they look at people whose values align with theirs and do their best to appeal to those people: their tribe. Behave like a brand and identify those people whose values align with yours and do your best to surround yourself with those people. We tend to emulate those around us. Once you eliminate negative attitudes and self-talk, it becomes easier to accept people for who they are - including yourself.

Accepting who you are, negative aspects included, it becomes a lot easier to stop comparing yourself to others.

Brushing off Compliments

It can be difficult to figure out sometimes whether a person means it when they offer us a compliment. However wrongly, we react in a way that affirms, in our minds, how humble we are.

The problem is that we're not being humble; we're merely undermining our own self-confidence.

Our typical reaction is to
- deflect the compliment to someone else
- be dismissive of ourselves
- assume that the compliment contains an ulterior motive
- point out an inherent weakness or flaw

Instead, we should learn to say, "Thank you" as graciously as you can and follow it up if necessary with an elaboration of how much you appreciate the other person's feedback.

Worrying

Worry is caused by living in the future, as it falsely appears to you now. It's useless and self-defeating. It also robs you of your influence over your own life, as it encourages you to think you have no control over events, which ultimately leads back to self-blame.

Living in the Past

It follows from not living in the future, that living in the past is going to cause you a lot of problems too. Constantly rethinking occasions when you were disappointed by other people or behaved badly does not allow you to move forward in life. Instead, it creates a behavior loop because your brain can't recognize imaginary events from real ones.

Lack of Self-Care/Self Harming

Going for days without washing, shaving, brushing your teeth, changing your clothes. Although self-neglect is an easy habit to fall into when you are depressed, it's just one more behavior pattern that makes you feel unworthy of success.

Make a point of spending just 20 minutes each day washing, cleaning and choosing attractive and comfortable clothing.

Lack of Sleep

Our brains require sleep to flush out toxins that build up around it during the day. Deep, regular sleep is an absolute must to prevent brain diseases such as Alzheimer's. Sleep is the perfect example of a habit because we fall into sleep patterns according to the decisions we make. Decide now to get a full 8 hours of sleep every night, and reap the rewards

Add New, Positive Habits
It's easier to stop bad habits by focusing more on creating newer positive ones. It's a little strange, but habits in one area of our lives tend to affect habits in other areas. Often, you'll find that setting better sleep patterns, or getting more exercise will energize you to start adding more positive behaviors.

While this list is by no means exhaustive, it covers many of the ways we fall into self-defeating behaviors and gives some indication of how to challenge them.

In general, to overcome any negative habits, it's best to

- allow some time for self-analysis
- focus on increasing positive habits

- change your behavioral reaction to triggers

Avoid Stop Gaps
Losing weight, gaining back hair, getting married. They'll all make you feel good in the interim. They may even solve part of your self-defeatist attitudes in the short term, but they only eliminate symptoms, not the disease. Real improvement requires consistent introspection and a willingness to be honest with yourself.

That's not to say that you shouldn't work on yourself by losing extra weight, getting fitter or romancing someone worthwhile. It's just important to understand that while such activities may improve those areas of your life, they're not to be mistaken for the complete solutions to your problems.

Wrap up

Don't be too alarmed by how many self-defeating behavior patterns that you have acquired. They may seem insurmountable, but when you break them down into a list of supporting habits and start addressing each habit – and build new ones – you'll find that taking positive action has a ripple effect in other areas of your life.

Having read this report, and spent some time on introspection, you should now have an understanding of how your behavior stems from your past, the uncomfortable emotions you try to avoid, and that it can be changed if you so choose.

Remember that some self-examination will be required. When you shine a light on one behavior, often others that lay hidden in darkness will also come into view.

Will power is certainly going to be required, because this process needs to come from within you. You can't expect someone else to sort out your behavior for you - it's yours.

But you can confide in someone close to you if you wish, and if that person is a positive force in your life, then that would be encouraged.

Stopping self-defeat may seem easy when you read it on paper, but if that were so it wouldn't sell so many books and courses. It's a complex issue that doesn't respond to cheerleading. It's symptomatic of a complex variety of internal conflicts between who you are, who you think you are and who you want to be.

Solving Your Self-Defeating Behavior: Checklist

Here's a checklist you can follow once you have internalized the idea that you are ultimately responsible for the continuation of your own self-defeating behavior.

1. Keep a diary of some sort. It needn't be a highly emotional, soul searching one. Just a few smiley face emoticons that help track the general progress of your emotions. There are apps like Evernote and Google Keep that allow the creation of checklists on your phone, so you can keep it private.
2. Determine which particular self-destructive behaviors seem to recur in your life.
3. Pay attention to accusations others make of your behavior, whether you think they are well founded or not.
4. Put some time aside once a week to look over your diary entries or checklist.

5. Look for anything that seems to rear its head on a regular basis. Examples might be, "drank more than I intended", "got angry when confronted about not helping around the house", "accused partner of not contributing to the household".

It may seem like a lot of trouble to go to, just to be able to recognize where your self-defeating behavior exists, but when dealing with a complex issue like this, it's best to put in the effort. Think of it like untangling a garden hose. It takes a little while to figure out which part is caught where, but once you figure that part out, unravelling it becomes a whole lot easier.

By investing time now to identify, accept and ultimately eliminate your self-defeating behaviors, you are setting yourself up for a much happier, fulfilling and successful life in the future. Start the work today! Good luck.

Inevitable

Developing An Unwavering Belief in Your Decisions and Actions

It's inevitable?

What does it mean when something is "inevitable"?

The Oxford dictionary defines the word as meaning "certain to happen; unavoidable." It's an impressive word, especially when you place it into the context of making decisions that lead to successful actions.

What we're talking about is becoming more certain of what we're doing. Think about this idea for a moment: what would your life be like if your decisions were so certain they would lead to the right thing to do at the right time?

Pretty amazing, right?

In this book, we're going to help you develop unwavering belief in your decisions and actions. We start by discussing the idea of believing in yourself. But we won't just talk about what self-belief is. We'll discuss why we lack self-belief and what happens to us when self-belief is gone.

From there, we'll visit the flip side of the idea and talk about the positive side of self-belief. You'll discover what happens when you believe in yourself and how this affects the decision-making process and the following actions.

Finally, we'll work through how you can develop this kind of certainty in your decisions and actions. Certainty means you can enjoy decisions that will inevitably be good, which in turn leads to the right action time and time again.

Do You Believe in Yourself?

What does it mean to believe in yourself? It shouldn't be a hard question, but we tend to struggle with it for some reason. When asked, most people would say they have confidence in themselves, but their actions don't always support it. This is why it's important to define the right terms before getting too involved in the rest of the book.

As we travel through this chapter, we're going to explore what self-belief is and why we lack it sometimes and what happens if this lack becomes chronic.

What is Self-Belief?

There are many different aspects to self-belief, making it impossible to define the phrase easily. It starts with a certain confidence in yourself which begins with how you think about yourself and manifests in what you do with these feelings. The key components of Self-Belief include:

A feeling you know what to do next
Trust in your abilities, intellect, creativity, etc.

Confidence in your actions
A certainty of success

There is no room for doubt in self-belief, nor does it accept failure. Not that you won't ever experience disasters in your life. You simply don't see them as stopping places. Instead, self-belief looks at mistakes as a means of learning new ways to do things. The important thing about self-belief, though, is the way it keeps going even when you falter or experience setbacks. Your confidence in yourself will always find a way to shine through again and pull you back up even when the going is tough.

Here's a pro-tip regarding self-belief: the more you feel good about who you are and what you're able to accomplish, the more confidence you'll grow. In other words, a strong self-belief tends to create more self-belief over time.

This is good news because this means you don't need a lot of self-belief to begin. You'll find out in chapter three, as even tiny leaps of faith can put you firmly onto the path of unwavering self-belief.

Why Do We Lack Self-Belief?

If self-belief is so wonderful to have, why don't we all have this kind of confidence all the time? Some of the answers might surprise you.

Life Experience
Depending on what you've gone through in life, you might have great self-belief or some real problems feeling good about yourself. Unfortunately, those who have experienced abuse or trauma, PTSD, or a lot of harsh criticism in their lives will very likely have issues with self-belief. We tend to internalize the negative messages around us far better than the compliments or kindnesses we receive.

Learning Experiences

We tend to forget how much those in authority over us can leave a lasting impact on our lives. When we are children, our parents and teachers become the most important people in our lives. We want to earn their praise and recognition, and so work hard to get it. But not everyone who has a child knows the right way to parent to be encouraging, and sadly some teachers don't belong in a classroom. What happens here is we start absorbing poor messages from these individuals who cast doubt on our abilities, our intellect, and even which predict our future success. Phrases like "You'll never amount to anything" or the more insidious "girls aren't good at math" can set up our expectations for failure.

Mass Media

If all the rest isn't already enough, then throw in what the world is ready to tell you about yourself. Suppose you're not thin, beautiful, rich, or a dozen other things. In that case, you're never going to amount to anything according to every commercial, movie, social media post, ad, or other form of mass communication. All you need to do is look at the celebrities to see how you don't measure up. Worse, even if you tell yourself these messages don't matter, try shopping for clothes sometimes. Every style on the rack seems designed to look great on one body type. But even this is okay...you just need to join a gym to attain that body. Right? It is everywhere.

Misinformation
Just when you thought you'd covered all the bases, you start hearing about the value of an unwavering self-belief coming from those around us. Our peers will be quick to point out those who appear to be confident as being 'stuck up,' 'full of themselves,' 'foolish' or 'boastful.' Why? Because people love to put down what they don't have themselves. The problem is, it's hard not to listen to this kind of talk or stay unaffected by it.

Physical Health
We are never at our best when we're not feeling well. If you're skipping meals, not getting enough sleep, or not getting exercise, your body eventually begins to suffer. Things like weight gain, chronic pain, or other health issues or disabilities will take a toll on self-belief. We start thinking our value is equated with our health, so the more we feel ill, the less confident we feel.

Mental Health
We don't always see ourselves clearly when we're having trouble with our mental health, either. Even small things like stress or lack of sleep can trigger depression or anxiety, both of which will drive down self-belief. This doesn't even consider more serious mental health issues such as being bipolar, suffering from borderline personality disorder, or other such illnesses. The problem here is we've been told for years our mental health is part of what gives us value, and we even joke about people who are 'crazy' or exhibit other such issues as though

they are something to be made fun of. It's no wonder people suffering from any of these issues start to see themselves as 'less than those around them.

The problem with all of these factors is just how little truth can be found in any of them. People who are unique, eccentric, depressed, anxious, neurotypical, neurodivergent, or anything else all can experience confidence and unwavering self-belief. These old messages need to take a hike, especially when you see what happens when you spend too much time believing them.

What Happens When We Don't Believe in Ourselves?

If you've ever found yourself thinking, "It doesn't matter what I think of myself," you're sadly mistaken. It does matter—a lot. The effects of not believing in yourself can be very serious, especially over the long term. Consider these factors. Notice how the negative aspects keep escalating. The longer you have problems with believing in yourself, the worse things will keep getting.

You Put Other People Down
When we feel bad about ourselves, it helps us feel better to think we're not at the bottom of the heap. Finding people who have it worse becomes a way of attempting to build yourself up. Even so, you have to admit there's

something kind of sad in saying, "Hey, at least I'm not a mess like that person over there," as a means of feeling good about yourself.

You Overreact to Criticism
The world is full of corrections. But sometimes criticism hurts, even when you have an unwavering belief in yourself. If your self-belief is suffering, though, criticism feels more like fault-finding. If you find yourself blowing up when people offer you advice, it might be because your negative self-belief has gotten in the way. The problem? Over time this will keep escalating until you can't hear a word from someone else without blowing up, costing you friendships and even putting your job in danger.

You Put Yourself Down When Things Go Right
When you succeed, you will almost always think of it as an accident when you have poor self-belief. This is why some people will make comments like, "Well, there can't have been many applicants" when they get a job or will deflect praise from others by belittling what you just did.

Your Work Suffers
It's hard to get things done when you're worried about doing it right, feeling like you're going to fail anyway, or even feel uncertain about the next steps and whether or not we're even doing the right thing. Also, when there's this much self-doubt, it's hard to put in your best effort. This means in work or school; you might have issues with productivity or quality of work.

You Quit Easily
When things go wrong, it only validates what you've always suspected: you're going to fail. You start thinking there's no point in trying again if this is the outcome you can expect.

You Ignore Opportunities
Opportunities are everywhere, from potential promotions at work to contest entries or new relationships just waiting to be developed. But when you don't have a strong self-belief, you'll likely ignore all of these. After all, why bother when you just know it's not going to work out if you're just going to screw it up anyway.

You Seek Validation

While validation isn't always a bad thing (after all, it's nice to be recognized), it can quickly become obsessive behavior. You start needing other people to reassure you, to tell you everything is fine. This is a double-edged sword, though, for much as you crave these kinds of compliments and affirmations, with poor self-image, you're never going to believe them. This puts you right back into the cycle of doing things to receive validation which might be harmful. This includes:

Caving to peer pressure
Letting other people decide things for you
Spending an excessive amount of time on social media
Agreeing with others even when you disagree
Trying to blend in with the crowd
Becoming sexual at a young age
Ignoring injustice

You Ignore Your Goals
Or you never make goals in the first place. Think about it. There's no point if you're never going to reach them. Why would you subject yourself to so much hard work for nothing?

You Withdraw from Your Friends
When you don't like yourself, it becomes impossible to think other people can see any kind of value in being your friend. As your self-belief grows more negative, it becomes more common to pull away from others or end relationships. Why? This kind of withdrawal is generally seen as a proactive measure to avoid being hurt. Sometimes we also see individuals pull away in other ways, such as deleting social media accounts or being abrasive with others hoping they will be the ones to end things.

You Fall into Escapism
When you don't like who you are, you become the last person you want to hang around with. Besides, with failed prospects, why even try to make goals, work on change, or otherwise put any effort into yourself? Instead, it becomes easier and easier to fall into drugs or excessive alcohol use as a means of not having to deal with your negative self-belief.

You Obsess About Changing
If you've ever wondered where eating disorders such as bulimia or anorexia come from, here's your answer. This strong dislike and dissatisfaction with who you are can turn into a strong desire to force change upon yourself. The problem? Much as you may be sculpting your outsides to fit an ideal, your faltering self-belief will never allow you to see yourself accurately or even to acknowledge what a beautiful person you already are.

You Have Issues with Depression or Anxiety
At some point, this negative self-belief takes root in such a way you start losing the way out. You see life as pointless or become fatalistic, thinking things will never get better. You run yourself down to where depression and/or anxiety sets in.

A Quick Self-Test

Are you worried you might be starting to experience the adverse effects of poor self-belief? Ask yourself these questions:

Are you checking your social media constantly for 'likes'?
Do you stand with your shoulders hunched in or otherwise try to make yourself physically smaller?
Do you cave in quickly during arguments to agree with the other person even when you know they're wrong?
Are you worried about impressing others?
Do you have a hard time taking constructive criticism?
Do you rehearse in your head what you want to say before saying it?
Do you put down others?
Do you have a hard time accepting compliments?

Do you make up excuses for why things went right?
Do you avoid being around other people because you're scared, they'll see you?
Do you obsess about making decisions, second-guessing yourself?
Do you procrastinate often?
In social situations, do you try to become invisible?
Do you hesitate to offer your opinion?
Do you give up very quickly when things go wrong?
Is your self-talk more negative than positive?
Does the idea of being alone with your thoughts scare you?
Do your friends think you overuse drugs or alcohol?

If you've answered yes to any of these questions, it's time to consider the alternative. Keep reading to discover the power of self-belief, followed by a chapter on how to develop an unwavering belief in yourself.

** Please note: If you find yourself struggling with depression, anxiety, or other recurring negative thoughts, there is help. Please consider talking to a health professional, counselor, or someone you trust. You don't have to deal with this alone!

Call 988 in the United States if you feel you are in crisis.

The Power of Self-Belief

By now, you have a clearer idea of just what self-belief is and how it affects you when you don't have it. Perhaps you're even wondering about what happens when you do believe in your actions and decisions. The answer is more amazing than you might think.

The power of self-belief is incredible, especially when you can harness it directly to create better decisions and amazing actions. Let's explore this idea by first discussing what your life would look like if you believed in yourself.

What if We Believed in Ourselves

How does this crazy kind of confidence change your life? In a word, it's better. Every aspect of your life is touched by unwavering self-belief, from how you relate to people around you, how you conduct yourself at work, and what you get out of your day. Don't believe it? Check out this list and see for yourself!

You Accomplish More
Just having the confidence to do something means you're more likely to get it done. After all, when we know something will be a success, we throw ourselves into the project without holding back.

You Have Self-Worth
Don't confuse this term with self-belief. Self-worth means you realize you have value as a human being. How does this translate in everyday life? You're not about to allow anyone to treat you badly—end of the story.

You Feel Good About the Future
You know you have the ability to set out and do what you want to do. This means you're already visualizing success.

You Feel More Capable
Are you faced with something complicated? When you have self-belief, you know you're up to it. You understand your abilities and skills, but you also know you have the capacity to learn. Challenge accepted!

You Feel More Positive
You know what you're capable of, you like who you are as a human being, and know you can make wise decisions. No wonder you're feeling good about life!

You're Healthier
This goes back to the idea of valuing yourself. Because you do, you're more likely to treat yourself well through exercise, diet, and yes, even getting enough rest at night.

You Make Your Own Decisions
When you lack self-belief, it can be hard to know the next best course of action. But when you're feeling more confident, this isn't the case. You don't need someone else to figure things out for you because you already know what to do.

You're Sexier
Haven't you heard? It's the confidence that attracts us to each other more than anything else. Self-belief also means you're not looking outside of yourself for validation, nor are you carrying baggage with you from previous relationships made up of all the negative things your ex said.

You're More Aware
We've talked about this before, but when self-belief is low, you tend to look inward a lot, focusing on the past, on negative self-talk, and on whatever else is plaguing you. With self-

belief, you have the confidence to quit spending time worrying so much about yourself and see what's going on in the world around you.

You're Ready to Change the World
When you have self-belief, you know you have value and feel like your efforts matter. This means you no longer give up when you see injustice but are more likely to take a stand and work to create change.

While all these things here include some great benefits, we have saved out the two most important. Self-belief makes a huge impact on the decisions we make and the actions we take. Keep reading to find out more.

The Benefits of Unwavering Belief in Our Decisions

All day long, we make decisions whether we realize it or not. Most of these are fairly small and feel mundane. They concern things such as what you're going to eat for lunch or the route you should take on the way to work. Occasionally we're hit with big life-changing decisions, such as deciding where to move to or what college to attend. Yet big or small, self-belief has the very same impact on how we go about making those decisions, and ultimately, on what we decide.

As you'll see here, the main benefit lies in making decisions thoughtfully without allowing self-doubt to keep you from becoming lost in the process.

The Decision-Making Process

Whenever you need to decide anything, there are certain steps that you need to take to make a wise and informed decision. Every one of these steps requires a certain level of confidence. Without it? Well, you'll see what happens in each step if you don't have an unwavering self-belief.

1. Have an Open Mind
When you have unwavering self-belief, this part should be fairly easy. It takes confidence to consider that you might have made a mistake, aren't seeing the whole problem, or missed something. Confident people understand they're human and don't shy away from their mistakes. As a result, they tend to be more willing to consider they might not know everything right off the bat.

What happens when you lack this confidence? There are several answers to this. Most people might feel so bad about thinking they've done something wrong; they shut down completely. They get caught up in beating themselves up and never see the potential solutions staring them in the face. Or they might become fearful of what other people might think of them if they're wrong and try to assign the blame somewhere else entirely. Neither of these actions is productive and can lead to impulsive and emotional decision-making.

2. Gather Information
The confident person understands they're still learning and growing and looks forward to discovering all the angles. They'll jump in to explore the matter until they feel comfortable that they have examined the problem thoroughly.

What happens when you lack this confidence? A person without self-belief will panic at this stage. They'll feel like they never have enough information and fall into the research aspect without ever surfacing for air again.

3. Explore the Options
The confident person has no problem thinking through different solutions, trying to see where each one will lead them. They know they can handle whatever twists and turns they encounter and are ready to challenge the outcome and discover what comes next.

What happens when you lack this confidence? The person without confidence might falter here, second-guessing themselves over and over again when it comes to trying to predict outcomes. Worse, they'll start predicting disaster for every single one of them, mostly because they're so sure they'll fail, they can't see any other outcome.

4. Ask Advice

Not every decision requires an outside opinion, but it's probably a good idea to have someone trusted weigh in before you make your final decision when faced with those big ideas. If you're confident, you won't be threatened by having someone else give their input but will be glad to be able to add their knowledge to your own. After all, you're comfortable with hearing differing thoughts, and since the final decision is still yours, you know you're still in control of the outcome.

What happens when you lack this confidence? When you lack confidence, this step is unpleasant. Someone else might make fun of your thoughts, think you're stupid, or otherwise put you down. Or worse, they'll laugh at you for even asking for help. In the worst-case scenarios, you might feel so threatened by the opinion of others that you will cave in to their opinion whether you agree with them or not, taking the decision out of your hands and putting it firmly under the control of someone else.

5. Act

We'll talk about this more in the next section. The final stage of this process is to make the decision and to act on it with confidence.

What happens when you lack this confidence? Without confidence, you'll probably go back over the steps a few more times, delay making the decision as long as possible, and even when you do make this decision, you'll second-guess it.

As a final note on this section, keep in mind having an unwavering belief in your action doesn't necessarily mean every decision is easy to make. There will come times when some decisions require a great deal of thought. The point being made here is how the confident person won't feel threatened by the process but can even look forward to it with practice.

The Benefits of Unwavering Belief in Our Actions

Of course, making decisions are only half the battle. As mentioned in the previous section, there comes a time when you need to act. Of course, you can make the best decisions in the world, but it's still worthless if you never push yourself into motion. You would think this wouldn't be the hard part, but it can be nearly impossible when you lack self-belief.

Consider what happens to your actions when you have an unwavering self-belief:

You know whatever you've decided is good for you, so you're eager to get to it.
You have certainty the outcome will be positive, either through giving you success or by giving you something you can learn from.
You know you'll experience positive emotional responses to the action. In short, you'll very

likely be happy or at least satisfied by the outcome.

You know you're doing something which will provide you with an opportunity to grow in new and exciting ways.

You recognize your actions are moving you further along the road to your goals and feel the excitement of making new progress.
You enjoy the confidence of being able to exercise your knowledge.

You realize there's no need to worry as you put your decisions into play.
You can relax. You've got this. There's no reason to stress.

How do you know these things? Simple. Because you've done the hard part of the work already, and you know you're making the right decision. You also understand what you're capable of and what the next steps are. This means you can relax and settle into doing the work laid out for you and be assured the outcome will be good no matter what.

Inevitable: Developing Unwavering Belief

Hopefully, by now, you're feeling a little excited about developing an unwavering belief in yourself. Imagine what life will be like when you do! Your decisions and actions will inevitably be exactly the right thing at the right time. With a life like this, it's easy to imagine success around every corner!'

It probably seems like this step is going to be a lot of hard work. The good news is this process isn't as difficult as you might think. Sure, you'll have to put a little thought into your actions, but soon these tips will become second nature, and you won't have to think about them at all. The trick is to think about these ideas as habits you want to build, which is nothing more than a matter of repetition over several days to set them in stone.

So, here's the process made simple:

Read through the list.
Try things that appeal to you.
Evaluate what you just did. Because everyone is different, some techniques might not work for you. Ignore those.
Keep practicing the tips which have proven to be the most helpful.

Also, you're going to want to do a self-check every so often, so you can catch when you might be faltering. Life can be difficult, and a bad day or an unkind word from someone can throw some self-doubt onto the most confident person. When this happens, spend a little time with these tips again until you feel like you're back and track and ready to take on the world.

Affirmations
There are certain things you need to hear if you want to have a strong belief in yourself. Start by

making up affirmations that remind you of how capable you are. Place these affirmations where you can't help but read them often.

Know What You Stand For

It's hard to have confidence if you don't know what values you hold or believe in. Take time to work through your system of beliefs. Not sure? Now is a great time to explore the issues and decide where you stand. As you build this confidence, you'll find you will start to feel more and more like you have something to say along with the courage to say it.

Accept the Flaws

It takes a strong individual to realize they aren't perfect. Try making a list of those areas where you know you need work. When you can face your limitations, you are fully accepting of who you are.

Change One Thing
This ties in with the last tip. When you fully understand who you are, you're going to see areas in your life where you need improvement. Rather than allow yourself to become caught up in these things, make a plan to change one thing about yourself. Dedicate the next few weeks to making this change.

Confront Fears
Anytime we allow our fears to rule us, we start holding back. This is where this tip is so important. Explore the causes of your fears and make a conscious decision to do something today which pushes your comfort zone a little and allows you to confront what you're afraid of.

Permit Yourself to Fail
When you have a good sense of what you're capable of, disaster doesn't take anything away from who you are. This gives you the freedom to move forward and make decisions that lead

to actions where the outcome isn't necessarily predetermined. This allows you to try new things in safety and freedom.

Embrace Uncertainty

When we lack confidence in our decisions, we can stall out easily and instead choose to do nothing at all. Sometimes the only way through this is to take a crazy leap of faith. Sometimes you just need to jump in and do whatever is in front of you. As you do, you'll start realizing you know what you're doing after all.

Keep Going

Anytime you slow down, it's easy to start doubting what you're doing or whether or not you're even doing the right thing. With this in mind, nothing builds confidence in your decisions than forward momentum. How to get this momentum? Simply do the next best thing. Then do the next best thing after that.

Keep Track of Accomplishments
How do you know you're doing well? If you keep a list of decisions that went well and actions you're proud of, you know right off just how good you are at making decisions. Unwavering self-belief is just a short step from there.

Take Care of Yourself
It's just about impossible to make decisions you can trust if you're exhausted or not feeling well. Sometimes the best thing we can do for our self-belief is to treat ourselves with respect by getting enough sleep, eating right, and exercising regularly.

Stand Up Straight
You'd be amazed at how much more confident you'll feel in everything you do just by adjusting your posture. Make a point to give yourself a posture check throughout the day and straighten your spine as needed.

Get to the Root of Your Doubts
What's holding you back? Rather than beating yourself up for negative thoughts, take some time right now to get to the bottom of them. Choose a negative thought which crops up often and hunt for the emotion at the base of it. Once you understand what's holding you back, it'll be much easier to lay it to rest.

Start Small
Big decisions can bring up many insecure feelings, especially if you've been struggling with self-belief. The best solution? Help yourself grow accustomed to decision-making by starting with the small choices and, as you gain confidence, working up to the bigger choices.

Learn Things
We never feel confident about decisions we make blindly. If you don't understand the problem or the possible choices, maybe it's time to stop and learn more about the problem. Doing your homework now will help you have

more faith in your choices and the actions that follow.

Write Out the Options
Making decisions can seem complicated, especially if you're trying to figure out something complicated. The easiest way to build confidence in your ability is to try writing down the options and the desired outcome. When you see things in black and white, it makes decisions easier and will help you feel good about your choice.

Get a Reality Check
How are you doing? When you struggle with self-belief, this can become very hard to answer. Things always appear much more negative than they are, but we just don't see it. Here's where a conversation with someone close to you can be invaluable. Ask them to help you remember some of your successes.

Change Up Your Surroundings
How can you keep negativity from taking over? Don't give it added ammunition. When we scatter too much stuff in our lives, we quickly become overwhelmed, unable to decide what to do next or how to go about doing it. To keep this kind of confusion out of your head, take the time to keep your surroundings neat, with the things you need most easy to find. Decisions come easier without all the clutter around you.

Validate Yourself
We've already talked about the dangers of looking for validation from others. If you want unwavering self-confidence, why not try validating yourself instead? Take a moment to be proud of a decision or action which you know you did well.

Do Something
Sometimes our self-doubts and negativity seem hard to defeat. We all have baggage, making it easy to dwell on past criticism or failure. When

this happens, sometimes all you need is a good distraction to help regain your confidence. Why not try exercising or an activity which makes you feel good. These will both help build back confidence quickly.

Look for the Lessons
Self-belief can take a nasty blow when you experience a setback. When this happens, rather than beating yourself up for failing, take the opportunity to figure out what you have gained from experience. The lessons learned will help you to make decisions you can count on.

Post the Good Stuff
Need a visual reminder of all the times you got it right? Why not write out your accomplishments on post-it notes and put them on every surface. Every time you find one of these notes, congratulate yourself on making a great decision or taking an awesome action and feel your confidence rise.

Check Your Logic

The next time negative thoughts start creeping in, take a minute to examine the statement when you're trying to figure out your next decision or action. For example, "I always fail at this" isn't logical. No one does anything the same way every time, so the word "always" is wrong. Replace false statements with truer ones, such as "I have succeeded at this several times."

Picture Yourself

How do you see yourself? When you have doubts, you're going to find that you focus on your flaws. In this exercise, close your eyes and picture all the things you like or admire about yourself. If you're having trouble finding positive traits, why not start with something you did which you're proud of. Remind yourself that you are still this person who has all these great features and makes wonderful decisions.

Take a Stand
The world is always ready to criticize. When you're uncertain in your self-belief, it's easy to agree, even though deep down you know what's being said isn't true. Use this exercise to step back. Remind yourself you have enough confidence to ignore what other people have to say. Then walk away. You don't need to listen to this kind of thing.

Embrace Life
When you want to have unwavering self-belief, don't forget this confidence comes with peace and joy. When you know who you are and what you're capable of, you really can relax and enjoy life. Not feeling it? Do something today which you truly love, which reminds you how awesome you are.

Of course, these are only a handful of ideas to get you started. The true key to building unwavering belief in your actions and decisions is to allow yourself to enjoy who you are as a human being. Accept the flaws while embracing the good. And always keep striving to grow, making new decisions, and taking action again every day of your life.

Wrap up

Can someone's belief in themselves be so strong that their decisions and actions inevitably lead to success? The answer, quite simply, is "yes."

In this book, you've learned a lot about self-belief. By now, you have a pretty clear understanding of what it means when you lose this belief. You also have come to see why it's so important to have and how to get it back when you're feeling down. Does this mean you're ready to face the world?

In fact, you are. Even if you're not where you want to be just yet, you will be the more you act on your thoughts and trust yourself to know what you're doing. After all, an unwavering belief in yourself is a work in progress. The more you try, the better you're going to get.

What's even more exciting is how much having this unwavering belief in yourself will change your world. You're going to start seeing more opportunities. You'll have confidence you know what you're doing, alongside the assurance you have what it takes to achieve your goals.

Success really is inevitable, after all!

The New You: The 7 Point Attitude Adjustment to Change Your Life

Introduction

Every individual on this Earth has their unique individual array of emotions, and those emotions reveal themselves in the form of distinct attitudes. How you use your short-term emotions determines your overall mood in life. So, that highlights the fact that people do have an active element of control over their happiness. And that's despite the fact that your mind is a powerful tool.

Of course, the attitudes that you hold are those that tend to come naturally, which means most people don't even realize how they're acting. Therefore, the first step is to identify the type of attitude you have and to be honest with yourself. Once you're aware of how you're projecting your emotions, you'll be in a better position to change.

Yes, it may be difficult, but in this eBook, we're going to discuss how you can adjust your attitude, so you lead a much more positive life. With a more positive life, comes increased happiness, flourishing relationships and enhanced performance in your career. Not only will we list methods to improve your attitude, but we'll also analyze both negative and positive attitudes, so you have a deeper understanding of how they present themselves.

The seven steps that we've compiled have been proven to be effective within every single age group, regardless of current situation or attitude. That's because they're versatile, and the tips we share with you can be molded around an individual and tailored to any scenario. As long as you're open to change and want that positive attitude, this eBook will be perfect for you.

Without further ado, let's delve in and restructure that attitude!

The Negative Attitude

We're going to start by discussing the negative attitude, as that's an area we want to address as quickly as possible. You see, a negative attitude can be present in a variety of different ways, so it can be difficult to label it as one specific thing. Everyone is programmed differently, and everyone goes through different experiences in life.

But it's not hard to recognize negative attitudes, and they don't just have an impact on your wellbeing, they affect others too. How? The bad energy that you emit when you're around others is contagious, and your negative attitudes can bring them crashing down.

Whether you accept it or not, having a negative attitude for a prolonged period can be extremely destructive, and can spiral out of control if left to its own devices.

Our brain was designed to help us through tough situations, which is why emotions show up so rapidly and why we can respond almost instantly. When we sense a real threat, it's the brain which activates the fight or flight response and prepares our body to take action. That action that is supposed to keep us safe.

However, when someone has a negative attitude (and hence negative thoughts), the part of our brain that controls the fight or flight response is effortlessly manipulated. What do we mean by that? Well, rather than responding to a real threat, those negative thoughts trick the brain into reacting in the same way even when there is no danger.

Subsequently, you'll experience all of the mental and physical symptoms of anxiety without any reason for them. For those who are living every day with a negative attitude, you'll most likely be familiar with the depressed state of mind, disinterest in attending social events, fragmented relationships with those closest to you, and an ever-present worry that is incredibly debilitating.

On top of that, you may also experience common physical side-effects, such as palpitations, difficulty breathing, hot sweats, dizziness, muscle tension, rapid heartbeat, and nausea. Living in a constant negative attitude impacts your physical health as well as your emotional health.

Most people who have a negative attitude trick themselves into thinking it's for the best. Have you ever thought:

- "If I expect the worst, I'll never be disappointed."
- "If I worry endlessly, I'll always be safe."
- "If I analyze this situation again, and again, and again, I'll be able to solve the problem."

The thing is, negative attitudes have the opposite effect. When you constantly fret about and expect the worst to happen, that anxiety can easily cloud your judgment and thinking. Your negative attitude makes it harder to problem-solve, creates imaginary scenarios that aren't real, and prevents you from challenging yourself to grow.

Your Negative Brain
Thinking negatively over a long period causes your brain to turn negative. Let's take a look at the parts of the brain that are affected by negative thoughts and feelings.

Amygdala: A significant catalyst behind negative attitudes is your past. Now, you should never let the past define you, but the part of the brain called the amygdala stores negative experiences. Unfortunately, that same part is responsible for triggering the fight or flight response. That means your prior negative experiences will cause your body to overreact to minor stress and instigate the fight or flight response.

Thalamus: Your thalamus works alongside the amygdala because it's this aspect of the brain that delivers sensory and motor signals around the body. Again, the thalamus doesn't comprehend the difference between negative thoughts and real danger.

Cortisol: Often referred to as the 'stress hormone,' elevated cortisol levels are the reason why negative attitudes stick around and don't budge. That's because cortisol can manufacture changes within your brain, and those changes increase the risk of developing long-lasting mental health disorders, such as generalized anxiety disorder, depression, OCD, ADHD, and schizophrenia. That highlights the importance of managing your negative attitudes because eventually, they could lead to more serious problems.

But there is good news! You can change your attitude! Thanks to groundbreaking work in the field of neuroscience, we now know that we can change our attitude if we are willing to work on it. We used to believe our brains were fixed, unchangeable once we entered adulthood. But research proves the plasticity of our brains, meaning we can change our thinking, which in turn, will change our attitude.

The Damage of Negativity
Though all of us fall into negative thoughts once in a while, consistently doing so means living a limited life due to fear and worry. Here are some ways that a negative attitude can severely hinder your happiness and success in life.

Fear of failure: There's no denying that nearly everyone has a fear of failure. But there's a fine line between using the fear of failure as motivation to work harder and using it as an excuse never to break free of your comfort zone. Those who are prone to the latter will struggle to progress in life because they'll never be willing to capitalize on opportunities handed to them.

Pessimism: Let's face it, we all know a person that is the typical 'glass-half-empty' type of individual. We also know how exhausting it can be to be in their company. Pessimism is always drawing on the negatives, rather than searching for the positives. In fact, many pessimistic people automatically pick out the one negative, even if there's an abundance of positives surrounding it.

Blaming others: It's much easier to blame others for your lack of happiness, rather than taking responsibility and accepting that you're in charge. People throughout your life could very well have caused you pain and distress, but it's your job to maintain your positivity. Dwelling on things and blaming others will not grant you happiness, so what's the point?

Assuming the worst: Worrying about bad things that could potentially happen is second nature to millions of people. But, for some people, it becomes an obsession. They are always conjuring up worst-case scenarios and wondering, "What if catastrophe strikes?" This thinking causes a substantial amount of stress. It's impossible to predict the future, and you'll never truly know what's going to happen. Although, the worst-case scenarios you imagine will rarely ever materialize.

Self-doubt: No-one is confident 24/7, 365 days of the year. Occasionally, you'll second-guess yourself and will need some reassurance. That's completely normal and appropriate. But, self-doubt becomes a negative attitude when you're always telling yourself you can't do something, you're not good enough, and you'll never achieve anything. Repeatedly having those thoughts will lead to unhappiness, because with those assumptions, you'll never test yourself to find out.

The Positive Attitude

You may be wondering why we focused on having a negative attitude first. As you're now probably aware, negative attitudes can send you to rock-bottom and then trap you there.

We wanted to show you how that attitude is doing more harm than just bumming you out on a daily basis. And we hoped this good, hard look would encourage you to take the powerful action required to commit to adopting a positive attitude. Now we are going to show you why taking that action is worth the effort.

A positive attitude can be the difference between having regrets later on in life and looking back thinking you've had a whale of a time. To help us explain further, honestly answer the following questions:

• Would you rather be the person who never took risks due to an immense fear of failure, or would you rather be the person who failed a few times but who eventually achieve their biggest goals?

- Would you rather be the person who needlessly complained because all they saw was negatives, or would you rather be the person who smiled at the positives in every situation?

- Would you rather be the person who wasted time blaming others for their hardship, or would you rather be the person who claimed responsibility, moved on and found true happiness?

We're guessing you'd choose the latter on every question, right? So, it makes sense to try your best to gain a positive attitude right now, rather than realizing the benefits when it's far too late. See, a positive attitude will enhance your life in ways that you'd never imagine, because it doesn't just affect you.

When you possess optimism, drive, resilience and all the other factions of positivity, you'll become happier in yourself, and others around you will tap into that positive energy. Essentially, a positive attitude has double the power. Yes, becoming happier in yourself is magnificent, but your happiness can increase even more if your loved ones are also full of positivity.

All you need to do is make some minor changes. There's a common misconception that positive people are a particular breed and somehow always make the right choices when it comes to handling their emotions. But a negative attitude forms when a person consistently gives in to the negative thoughts that naturally pop up. On the other hand, a positive attitude starts when a person makes a conscious effort to replace those negative thoughts with positive ones. So, all that it takes is some effort. You need to put negative thoughts to the back of your mind and strive to find the positive in any situation.

Positive Attitude and Your Health

We mentioned the way a negative attitude impacts your health, so let's turn that on its head and look at the ways a positive attitude benefits your physical health.

Less stress: The most obvious benefit of having a positive attitude is a reduction of stress and lower levels of cortisol running through your body. Less stress in your life is a much bigger deal than you may assume. You'll have a lot more energy, you'll get better sleep, you'll smile a lot more, and you'll be a lot stronger mentally. Plus, less stress will allow you to perform to a much higher standard because your mind will be a lot clearer.

Stronger immune system: No, a positive attitude is not a replacement for vitamin C, but it can have similar effects. A countless number of studies have proved that the body and mind have a very tight-knit connection, which is why negative thoughts often bring about a ton of physical symptoms. Moreover, a positive attitude not only removes those physical symptoms, but it also strengthens the immune system and so cuts down the number of illnesses you contract.

More happiness: Who doesn't want to be happy? We don't think you'll find anyone on this Earth that will tell you they love being stressed, depressed, or disinterested. Happiness comes from within, and a positive attitude will allow you to see the bright side of life. If you look at everything from a positive perspective, you're bound to feel happier than those who don't.

Benefits of a Positive Attitude

If the benefits of your physical health weren't enough to make you rethink the way you live, we've included other ways a positive attitude makes life easier and more enjoyable.

Open-minded: Change is inevitable in life. When you grow older, as the workplace evolves, and as different situations occur, your life is bound to change. But those who are positive will remain open-minded to these changes and embrace them with open arms. As a result, they're empowered to prosper and maintain strong performances while other people struggle to cope with the mental pressure.

Determined: Determination is an excellent trait to have, because persevering towards your goals, regardless of setbacks and stress, is the only way to succeed. Successful regarding their career and their happiness. The key to being determined is figuring out what's going to make you happy because aimless determination won't lead to overall positivity.

Kind: Positive people can get along with others with ease, which means they can then form rewarding relationships and effective connections. But the way they do that isn't rocket science, it's just through acting kind, using basic manners and being approachable. You'll find that being kind brings you a lot more happiness than being negative does so ensure you're always trying to be as friendly as possible.

Resilient: Negative people tend to take things to heart, which is why they moan, complain, and worry so much. On the other hand, positive people possess a high level of resiliency, which enables them to withstand criticism, overcome failure and perform under pressure. There's no avoiding difficult situations in life, but it's better to brush them off and keep moving forward.

Understand other points of view: Another aspect of having a positive attitude that goes a long, long way is understanding other points of view. With that, you can evade an awful lot of conflict, arguments, and broken relationships. Although, understanding other points of view doesn't mean straying from your own beliefs. It just means not enforcing them aggressively. Listen carefully and respond in a way that doesn't cause negative emotions, that's all.

The 7 Point Attitude Adjustment

By now, I bet you're raring to put negative attitudes behind you and start attaining some positive ones, right? After all, there's no better way to make the most out of your life than to adopt some positive thinking, rather than waste time being and feeling negative.

Luckily for you, we've constructed an awesome strategy which will drastically improve your attitude – The 7 Point Attitude Adjustment. If you absorb all of the knowledge and put the ideas into practice, you – and those around you – will notice a huge change for the better. But let us reiterate, you must take control of your own life and make these changes yourself.

Think Positive Thoughts

The art of acquiring positive energy is to start thinking positive thoughts. If you're naturally a negative person, you might find this difficult in the beginning. That's why it's imperative that you make a conscious effort to correct yourself whenever you're having negative thoughts. Again, this may be a struggle as you may not even realize you're negative, but over time it'll become easier.

A super tactic to deploy when trying to enhance your mindset is to seek the support of those around you. Unquestionably, it's solely your responsibility to replace your negative thoughts with positive ones, but you can call on your loved ones and peers to help you spot when you're negative. For instance, if one of your negative attitudes is to be pessimistic when you're in the workplace, ask one of your trusted colleagues to remind you that you're working on becoming more optimistic.

Another method you can use is always to remember what you have to be grateful for in life. That's a fantastic approach for two reasons. The first is that when you celebrate all of the positive things in your life, you'll gradually become happier in your everyday life. You'll start to walk around with a smile knowing things are amazing and could be much, much worse. Subsequently, by actively thinking about all the wonderful things in your life, you'll build some resilience.

That means when you are having a tough time, and plagued with negative emotions, feelings, and thoughts, you'll have that automatic buffer which will reduce the effect they have on you. Even if you find it impossible to remove those negative thoughts, you can start focusing on all the positive things that you have to be grateful for in your life.

Lastly, a big tip that we can provide you with is thinking of the potential for a positive outcome and believe it will happen. As the Dalai Lama once stated – "See the positive side, the potential, and make an effort," which applies perfectly. Just because you're trying to think positive thoughts, doesn't mean you'll always find some.

But, if you can find the potential for positivity instead, you'll find that the next progression is to discover the positive thoughts that go with it. For example, if you're assuming you're going to get fired if you don't complete a task, try to replace that with the thought of your boss giving you another chance. Following that, you can then logically think that you're not going to get fired because you're brilliant at your job.

Just think, if your mind can conjure up a multitude of negative thoughts, it can do the same thing with positive thoughts. You've just got to search for the positive in every situation, which will flow into your brain seamlessly the more you practice.

Create Your Happiness

Too many people have the belief that the world owes them something. But, no, the world doesn't owe you anything, and just being alive is a blessing. Regarding forging a successful career, creating a beautiful family and obtaining true happiness, that's on you. When you thrive on the pressure of creating your happiness, you'll make much more progress and stop feeling so sorry for yourself.

That may sound like a harsh lecture, but no other human being can take responsibility for your happiness. Fortunately, there are a plethora of things you can do to create that happiness, and it isn't that difficult.

At the end of the day – before you do anything else – you need to find what makes you happy.

Is it visiting your family where there's no shortage of love, positive vibes, and laughter? Is it walking your dog around the park as the sun sets in the background? Is it playing your favorite video game with your favorite music playing?

Alternatively, it may be individual people that make you happy. Is it seeing your wife smile when you fetch her that cup of coffee? Whatever it is that makes you happy you need to try and fill every day with it. Apologies for stating the obvious but doing small things that make you happy will, in turn, increase your overall happiness.

Another way to create your happiness is to make yourself a priority. It's a tendency among people with negative attitudes to care too much about what other people think. So, they'll neglect all of the things that make them happy, to do things that aid someone else's happiness. But, believe us, that isn't productive. You'll end up feeling depressed and surrounded by people that don't care about you.

A better option is to put yourself first and become happy with yourself first. Once you've done that, you'll start attracting people that love you for who you are and are content just with being in your presence. Ask yourself – do you want to share your time with people that you have to sacrifice your wellbeing to make them happy? You have a super personality with plenty to offer, so don't put up with people who want to take you for granted.

How do you put yourself first? Easy, take naps when you want them, go for a massage when you want one or watch a film on your own when you want to. You could even try new things, like hiking up a mountain to enjoy nature and feel the thrill of accomplishing something that you never thought was possible.

Boost Your Personal Energy

Personal energy is something that people neglect all the time, and some people have never even heard of it. When people are feeling tired all the time, feeling under the weather or feeling like their performance levels have dipped, they always look to physical ailments and general stress.

Off the back of those, people start to develop negative attitudes as they don't feel like their usual selves. But a massive cause is low energy levels, and that is resolvable with some small tweaks. Hydration is a large component of energy, and it's no secret that the majority of the population don't drink the required amount of water on a daily basis.

If you start by hitting the average amount needed per day, you'll notice a huge boost in energy and mood. For those that find it difficult to keep drinking throughout the day, try sourcing a large water bottle that tells you how much you've drunk. The obvious point to coincide with that is to ensure you're making an effort to keep drinking and keep filling it up.

Moving on, another method to lift your energy levels is to take power naps when you notice your performance dipping. For some people who work the traditional nine-to-five, that will be a bit trickier. Try shutting your office door, turning off the lights and laying on the floor behind your desk. No one will see you, and it will make a huge difference in how you feel. No office? Try closing your eyes and resting in the break room or your car during your lunch hour. Just set the alarm on your phone and relax. All it takes is a quick 20-30 minutes to rejuvenate your body and mind.

On the subject of sleep, an idea to make you feel fresher each day is to wake up at the same time, preferably as early as possible. If you start your day much earlier than you're used to, you'll be able to be a lot more productive and won't feel like you're wasting time by sleeping in too long. When it comes to your attire, try wearing brighter colors rather than the dull, neutral ones all the time.

Your clothes match your mood, so brighter colors will help significantly to achieve a positive attitude. The last two tips are related to health. First, if you're a smoker then do all you can to quit, as that will dramatically boost your energy and reduce your risk of developing a chronic disease.

Secondly, try to divide your meals up into smaller portions, so they're less taxing on your digestive system, and ensure your diet is balanced. When you starve yourself, it's easy to become grumpy, and then when you eat a large meal, your body will snatch all of your energy to digest your food.

Believe in Yourself

So many people either approach a situation assuming they're not good enough, or they thrive off of the belief that others have in them. Neither of those is optimal as your performance and happiness truly derive from within, and unless you believe in yourself, you'll never achieve a high level of either of those.

Sometimes it may be difficult to believe in yourself, but it's crucial that you find a way. We're not going to leave you to do that alone, and we'll help you out. The first way to enhance the belief in yourself is to assess your past success. If you've had successful experiences before – no matter what it was – you'll know you're capable of achieving great things again.

You can be of any age to do that, as success means different things to different people. For example, if you've overcome all of the stress of an exam and received high scores, you'll know pressure won't defeat you. Ultimately, the belief in yourself will sky-rocket if you know you've been in a tough situation in the past and succeeded.

Another method is to trust in your ability, because if you have specialist skills in a certain area you know you'll be able to perform highly. For instance, let's say you have a basketball trial approaching, and you're just assuming that everyone else there is going to be better than you. If you can be confident in the skills you have, you'll be in a much better position to succeed.

Your ability is there. You need to condition your mind to be positive so that nothing stops you from flourishing. Just think, would you have signed up for the trial if you thought you would fail? No, so deep down you do believe in yourself, you need to bring that to the forefront of your mind.

If you're still seriously struggling to believe in yourself, then a superb option is to seek the expertise of a qualified life coach. They're trained to identify strengths in people, and then to make them acknowledge those strengths. They'll stay with you every step of the way providing support and guidance. If you ever start to doubt yourself, they'll find ways to remind you of past successes and make you focus on your immediate goals. Generally, they'll believe in you, so eventually, you start believing in yourself.

Worry Less

We all worry from time to time, but some people worry non-stop which is very unhealthy. Not only will it bring about all of those negative feelings and physical symptoms, but you'll never really gain anything from worrying. It's just wasted energy. Worrying is being extremely apprehensive about what's going to happen in the future or about a problem that's already present.

Constant overthinking makes you feel like you're in control, but your mind will only create more problems that aren't there. Additionally, worrying will only lead to more worrying, because you'll always find worst-case scenarios that could potentially happen, but are very unlikely. We're not saying stop worrying altogether, because that's not realistic.

But it's vital to distinguish normal worrying from excessive worrying. For instance, worrying about your child going out on their own for the first time is acceptable, because you want them to be safe. However, frequently checking for lumps and bumps and worrying that you have a serious health risk all the time is not acceptable.

Worrying less is far from an easy feat, though. Most of the time worrying is a natural reaction, and the more you try to not think about it, the more it haunts you. The negative thinking keeps on increasing, and the worst-case scenarios and second-guessing yourself keep on multiplying. Why do you think millions of people suffer from mental health issues each year? Because the negative thoughts are so hard to eliminate, but it's possible so don't give up!

The idea is not to try and stop the worrying cycle. Instead, give yourself a period where you can worry till you're exhausted. When you permit yourself to worry, but only during a specified period, you'll retain control and won't aggravate the thoughts by trying to suppress them. Just make sure the period you select isn't too long – half an hour would suffice.

It's not uncommon for thoughts to become clouded and fuzzy during excessive worry, so a way to combat that is to write your worries down. When you've got all of your fears down on a piece of paper, you'll realize how out of proportion they've become. If you need to address any severe problems, you can deal with them logically rather than overthinking and making things worse.

Another method is to accept your situation and give control away. Endlessly worrying won't change the outcome, so there's no benefit whatsoever to worrying and working yourself up for no reason. So, try to limit your worries and let time prove to you that the outcomes you imagine never occur. Negative thoughts are worlds apart from actual reality.

Conquer Your Fears

A terrific way to enhance your attitude and tilt it towards the positive side is to do your utmost to conquer your fears. Fears are something that everyone has, but something that no-one wants.

It doesn't matter what fear you have; the first step is acknowledging it. Too many people are in denial and want to fuel their ego rather than admit they're honestly scared of something. But, by doing that, you'll never be able to overcome it because you'll never actually believe there's a problem to solve.

Once you understand your anxiety, you can then go ahead and work on conquering it. The next step in that is exposing yourself to it. That may trigger some instant anxiety, but there's nothing to worry about here. When you expose yourself to the anxiety and then conquer it, you'll never look back.

Let's use the fear of failure as an example. If you never take risks and challenge yourself to progress due to the fear of failure, you'll need to discover a potential risky opportunity. Normally, you'd decline, right? But we want you to accept the opportunity and do all you can to make it a success. It may be a surprise to you, but you'll notice that nothing bad happens – the world doesn't end!

In fact, you might find that you achieve much more than could have ever dreamed. Although to fully conquer your fears, you've got to expose yourself to them more than once. When you repeatedly face and overcome your fears, you'll eventually eradicate the anxiety so that it's no longer a fear.

When you are conquering your fears, there are ways to improve your chances of success, though. Over the years plenty of expert studies have reported that positive visualization techniques help massively with performance. Before facing the fear, if you consistently imagine the situation going well, then you'll attack it with a much more positive frame of mind.

There's always the possibility of the situation not going as planned, so you also need to concentrate on conditioning your mind to cope with any stress. If you jump into the situation with positivity but acknowledge that you may experience negative emotions, you'll conquer your fears in no time at all. To manage your stress, try deep breathing, meditation, and regular exercises. If you're mentally strong, you'll perform better.

Overcome Negativity in Others

Throughout this eBook, there have been regular mentions of your attitude not only affecting you but also affecting those around you. But that works both ways. If your peer group is stocked full of negative individuals who do nothing more than constantly paint life in a negative light, that will naturally impact your attitude.

As humans, we're influenced all the time by things that are going on around us. However, it's your responsibility to do something about it and escape from the negative aura. You might assume that we're going to tell you to run for the hills to avoid ever coming into contact with those people, but we don't live in a perfect world.

There are times when you'll have to learn to overcome the negativity of others and be positive when the odds are against you. The first tip to do that is to respond instead of reacting. Reacting is where you let your instincts take over, and you let all of those negative emotions that are built up inside of you pour out. The trouble with reacting is that you don't have time to acknowledge the consequences of your actions, so it will just make things ten times worse.

When you respond, you give yourself time to think, remain calm and assess what will happen. In that case, you can deal with the facts rather than the emotions. What we mean by that is, instead of focusing on all of the emotions that are both in the air, and developing inside your head, focus on the details of the situation. If you start to let the negativity get inside your head, your attitude will plummet, and that's when your happiness starts to decrease.

For instance, if a colleague is telling you that your tactics will never work, your gut might tell you to shout, scream and give them a piece of your mind. But what will that achieve? Nothing! So, you can listen to what they've got to say, explain how your tactics could work, and then inform them that if they don't work, you'll find another solution.

Despite other people being negative, you always have control over your attitude. That means if people are shooting your ideas down or not listening to your suggestions, you still have the power to adopt a positive attitude and be the bigger person.

There you have it, a simple 7-step guide to turning your frown upside down and catapulting it into the upper realms of happiness. Like we've already touched on, though, some people will never obtain a positive attitude and improve their lives for the better because they'll read and never take action.

Things will only change if you have a deep desire to change them, and you're willing to do everything you can to use the guidance given. Trust us, these seven steps will work wonders for you, but only if you commit to them and start implementing them every single day.

Self Acceptance

When you think of having good emotional health, terms like happiness, self-esteem, self-confidence, optimism, and mental toughness likely come to mind. You might not consider the ideas of self-acceptance and contentment.

But isn't contentment what we're all seeking?

Contentment is the place where we don't need anything. We're completely satisfied as we are, as our life is.

Think of how many things you do each day in an effort to feel more content:

- You say or do things to impress others.

- You say or do things to avoid being ridiculed by others.

- You work at a job you don't like so you can make more money to buy things you want or to impress others.

- You exercise and diet beyond what is reasonable in order to look a certain way.

The list is really endless. We spend a lot of our day trying to feel more content. However, these things aren't the path to radical contentment.

The real secret is self-acceptance.

"The truth is: Belonging starts with self-acceptance. Your level of belonging, in fact, can never be greater than your level of self-acceptance, because believing that you're enough is what gives you the courage to be authentic, vulnerable and imperfect."

– Brene Brown

WHAT IS SELF-ACCEPTANCE?

There are many ways to look at self-acceptance. Some of them are more constructive than others. It would be a mistake to think of self-acceptance as a blanket acceptance of your weaknesses, bad habits, and negative tendencies in the absence of any responsibility to continue to improve.

Self-acceptance isn't an excuse for laziness and complacency. You can be content and still advocate self-improvement.

It also doesn't mean that you accept your fate and determine that nothing can or should be done to change your life.

Self-acceptance is a reckoning with yourself. It's an acknowledgement of your shortcomings, character, strengths, habits, and tendencies. It's about facing the truth and accepting that reality. Once you know where you are, you can make a reasonable plan to move forward.

Self-acceptance ultimately leads to contentment because you are no longer fighting with yourself. Because let's face it, you cannot be both your #1 fan and your #1 enemy. It's self-defeating.

You need to free yourself from self-punishment in order to be healed. When you release yourself from the negative thoughts that hold you back – and accept where you're at – you are setting yourself on a truly radical journey toward contentment, peace, and happiness.

But that's easier said than done. In the next section, we'll explore the reasons why self-acceptance can be so challenging.

"For me, art really starts with acceptance, self-trust. Wherever you come to with art, it's perfect. You don't have to come with anything. What you bring to something is the art. That's where it's found. It's found within you."

— Jeff Koons

WHY ACCEPTING YOURSELF IS SO CHALLENGING

We're hard on ourselves. Many of us are more understanding and forgiving of others than we are of ourselves. It doesn't make a lot of sense. If anyone is going to be on your side, it should be you!
There are several common signs that you're being too hard on yourself:

1. You dwell on your mistakes. This accomplishes nothing positive. It does

accomplish several things that are negative. Avoid doing this.

o   We're all human and make mistakes. Dwelling on mistakes makes you feel less capable and miserable in general.

2.   You compare yourself to others. There's always someone richer, better looking, more musically talented, "luckier," or has children that do better in school.

o   Comparing yourself to others is dangerous. You don't know the other person's background or available resources. They may have a huge advantage.

o   You're also more likely to compare yourself to exceptional people. Do you compare your looks to the middle-aged man or woman at work that has three kids? Of course not! You compare yourself to the 21-year-old intern that models on the side.

3.   You don't give your own ideas a fair chance. How many great ideas have you had, but ultimately dismissed?

4.   You spend too much time thinking about your past failures. Oh, the past. You chickened out and didn't ask Mary to prom. Or you majored in liberal arts instead of engineering. Maybe you didn't get that dream job. There's always something.

o   If you focus on negative experiences, you're failing to accept yourself and your current reality.

5.   You can't take a compliment well. There are good things about you. It's okay when others acknowledge those things. Your inability to accept a compliment from others is a sign that you don't accept yourself.

6. You're unrealistic. Being unrealistic might be seen as being kind to yourself, but it's not. If you truly don't have what it takes to become an NBA star, or a Rhodes Scholar, or a CEO, you're not doing yourself any favors by holding onto unrealistic expectations. You're ultimately being hard on yourself.

It's not easy to accept yourself. We've been taught that the ideal person is financially successful, athletic, attractive, cool under pressure, hilarious, creative, and the life of the party. Most of us will never check all of those boxes.

There are many signs that you're not as accepting of yourself as you could be. Be on the lookout for these signs. You probably don't accept yourself as much as you think!

"Acceptance of one's life has nothing to do with resignation; it does not mean running away from the struggle. On the contrary, it means accepting it as it comes, with all the handicaps of heredity, of suffering, of psychological complexes and injustices."

– Paul Tournier

9 WAYS TO BEGIN ACCEPTING YOURSELF

Accepting yourself is a process. It's a habit. The little things you do, or fail to do, each day determine your level of self-acceptance. Developing these useful habits and dropping the negative habits is a huge step in the right direction. It's hard to accept yourself any other way.

Be accepting of yourself each and every day by making these actions habits:

1. Let go of your mistakes and failures. Take the necessary time to learn from your negative experiences. Once you've done that, there's nothing else to be gained by them. Let them go.

   o Decide how you can avoid making the same error in the future. Then move on.

2.   Only compare yourself to yourself. Comparing yourself to someone else is like comparing a tree to a loaf of bread. There's no comparison. However, you can compare yourself to your previous results.

o   If you're doing "better," you have every right to be excited.

o   If you're coming up short, be excited that you know you can easily rectify the situation.

3.   Separate yourself from your emotions. Your emotions are separate from you. They are something that you're experiencing, just like someone stepping on your toe. Observe them as a feeling in your body, or as a piece of paper blowing down the street. Just observe them.

o   A piece of paper blowing by doesn't have any control over you. Your emotions don't have to control you either.

4. Be aware of what makes you unique and embrace it. It might be your flaming red hair, your incredible IQ, or your compassion for animals. Maybe you're in the bottom 5th percentile for height. You're not exactly the same as anyone else.

o It's your uniqueness that potentially provides the most value to you and the world.

5. Let go of the things you can't change or control. You're not accepting of your life or your limitations if you worry about those things beyond your influence.

o Ask yourself, "Is there anything I can do about this?" If not, there's no reason to dwell on it.

6. Do something that you've always wanted to do. Avoid denying your impulses. If you've always wanted to learn how to play the bagpipes or write a sappy screenplay, now is the

time. When you deny your healthy impulses, you're not accepting yourself.

7. Be more assertive. Let people know what you think. Give your opinion. Allow your voice to be heard. Do the things you want to do. Assertiveness is a form of honesty - about you and your own desires.

8. Recognize your thoughts and feelings. Examine your self-talk. Stand in front of a full-length mirror and take a good look at yourself. Notice your thoughts throughout the day. Acknowledge how you judge yourself.

o Most people distract themselves with TV, the internet, food, their smartphone, or some other strategy. This is to avoid spending time with themselves. Turn off the distractions and notice what happens.

9. Continue evolving. Those with little self-acceptance tend to be stuck. They can't move

toward anything positive. Be honest with yourself about what you like and dislike and allow your life to evolve.

Treat each day as a new opportunity to practice self-acceptance. You must choose self-acceptance if you want to experience it firsthand. It won't happen by accident. Develop self-acceptance habits and drop your tendency to judge yourself harshly. Free yourself from your emotions.

"I think happiness comes from self-acceptance. We all try different things, and we find some comfortable sense of who we are. We look at our parents and learn and grow and move on. We change."

– Jamie Lee Curtis

SELF-ESTEEM AND SELF-CONFIDENCE

You can be aware of your shortcomings and still be happy with yourself. Your self-confidence doesn't have to suffer either. You can be honest with yourself and still be a powerful force in the world.

You might be thinking, "I thought I was supposed to be honest with myself, not build myself up."

This is being honest with yourself. If you had a truly accurate picture of yourself and your situation, you'd be a lot happier with yourself and a lot more excited about life in general!

Build self-esteem and self-confidence simultaneously with these strategies:

1. List your greatest successes. Remember when you were at your best. Remind yourself how that felt.

2. Make a list of the things you appreciate about yourself. List three things each evening. See just how great you really are.

3. Dress up. You walk a little taller when you're wearing your nice clothes. You deserve to feel good. There's no reason to wait for a job interview, wedding, or funeral to look or feel your best.

4. Live by your values. When you live by your code, you feel good about yourself. You feel bad when you do the opposite.

5. Set a small goal and achieve it. Give yourself an easy path to feeling good and enhancing your life. Set an easy goal and taste success.

6. Be kinder toward others. If you're hard on others, you're probably hard on yourself, too.

Avoid saying anything negative and be a good listener. That will get you 90% of the way there.

If you have sufficient self-esteem and self-confidence, self-acceptance is easier to find. You're already pretty great, so there's no reason not to recognize it. Treat yourself with the admiration and respect that you deserve.

"In my research, I've interviewed a lot of people who never fit in, who are what you might call 'different': scientists, artists, thinkers. And if you drop down deep into their work and who they are, there is a tremendous amount of self-acceptance."

– Brene Brown

MEDITATION AS A TOOL FOR SELF-ACCEPTANCE

Meditation and mindfulness are all the rage these days. Though they have been around for several thousands of years, they have enjoyed a new level of popularity. Even the scientific world is getting involved. A quick search on your favorite search engine will demonstrate just how interested the world is in these topics.

While meditation accomplishes many things, we're interested in self-acceptance. Meditation is a powerful method of stripping away the extraneous garbage that stands in the way of realizing the truth.

Meditation allows you to see your erroneous thoughts and beliefs more easily. It also provides more emotional control. When your emotions are appropriate, and proportionate, it's easier to accept yourself and others.

"When you are discontent, you always want more, more, more. Your desire can never be satisfied. But when you practice contentment, you can say to yourself, 'Oh yes - I already have everything that I really need."

– Dalai Lama

Follow these tips to incorporate a daily meditation practice into your life:

1. Create a daily schedule you can keep. It's much better to meditate each day for a few minutes than to meditate for longer periods of time a couple of times a week. Be realistic. Ideally, you can set aside at least 20 minutes a day.

o Avoid the mistake of failing to schedule your meditation time. If you wait until you have time, you'll never do it.

2. Find a comfortable spot. You don't need much. Any quiet spot where you won't be disturbed will work just fine. A firm chair or a seated position on the floor will work. Lying down can even work, provided you can stay awake!

3. Start small. It's more challenging to sit with yourself for 20 minutes than you think. Five to ten minutes is a good start.

4. Meditation is a relationship with yourself. So, be nice to yourself. It's about self-acceptance and compassion for yourself.

5. Focus on your breathing. Feel the air moving in and out of your body. Feel the sensation of the air moving past the edges of your nostrils.

6. Continue until your mind wanders. You probably won't even catch yourself the first several times your mind drifts away. All of

sudden, you'll realize that you've been thinking about work, school, dinner, or your neighbor's annoying dog.

7. When your mind wanders, let those thoughts go. Think of thoughts as clouds blowing by. You don't have to pay attention to them or be affected by them. Just allow them to pass through your attention and return your attention to your breath.

o Your mind will wander a lot at first. You might not even be able to last 30 seconds before your mind is off to another place. That's okay. Just keep going. You'll get much better with practice.

Meditation will show you that your mind creates thoughts. These thoughts lead to feelings and beliefs.

You'll also learn that you don't have to be affected by them. Being upset by your thoughts is a little like punching yourself in the face. Unclench that fist by allowing your thoughts to pass on through.

Most people spend so much time "thinking" and being influenced by their thoughts, they have a weak grasp of reality. The world is going on around you, not inside your head. You'll have a more honest perspective of yourself, the world, and those around you if you can quiet your mind.

You'll quickly learn to avoid being bothered by your thoughts. They'll move along on their own, provided you don't engage with them.

This is crucial to contentment. When you're not being energized by your extraneous thoughts, you'll experience real peace. When something negative happens, the event isn't the real issue, it's all the thoughts that run through your head.

Learn to deal effectively with your thoughts, and you can easily push past any self-doubts that keep you from accepting yourself and finding contentment.

"Health is the greatest possession. Contentment is the greatest treasure. Confidence is the greatest friend. Non-being is the greatest joy."

– Lao Tzu

Developing Self-Awareness

Self-awareness is the most important aspect of personal development. It determines nearly everything else, including whether you're able to stay motivated and achieve your goals. As you peel away the layers, you'll discover wonderful things about yourself when you simply become more aware.

With self-awareness, you can change deeply held beliefs if they don't serve you well. The journey of self-discovery is never-ending and filled with surprises and adventures in your inner landscape.

When you become self-aware, you know your strengths, weaknesses, and personality type. But it's more than this. Fully knowing yourself includes being aware of your thoughts and watching them objectively as an observer, without emotion or attachment.

For example, you might tell yourself, "Now I'm experiencing anger." You can then go on to ask yourself why you're getting angry and where that anger is coming from. Certainly, your soul within you is not angry. So who is?

"To have greater self-awareness or understanding

means to have a better grasp of reality."

- Dalai Lama

Discover Your True Self

Go deeper into yourself and peel away the layers until you can see who you truly are. This is the sort of analysis and probing that will help you answer the question that great minds have asked across the centuries: "Who am I?"

You may be an artist, but that's only the face you show to the world. Identification as an artist can create limitations, too. By defining who you are, you may categorize yourself and put yourself in a "box."

For example, a commonly held belief about artists is that they can't or don't make much money. Do you want to define yourself that narrowly?

As you explore yourself, you'll discover that you're capable of transforming yourself and creating your own world.

You'll be able to see yourself as you really are. You can either try to escape from this knowledge, or welcome it with open arms as an opportunity for self development.

If you welcome it, you could change the traits you dislike and build on those traits you do like. Frequently, we have behaviors left over from childhood that served us well then, but don't work well for us as adults.

"A human being has so many skins inside, covering the depths of the heart.

We know so many things, but we don't know ourselves! Why, thirty or forty skins

or hides, as thick and hard as an ox's or bear's, cover the soul.

Go into your own ground and learn to know yourself there."

- Meister Eckhart

Turn the Spotlight Within

The only person you can change is yourself. When you choose to transform yourself, you'll notice changes in your environment, including in the people who surround you. The world is your mirror and both the negative and the positive situations you encounter are created by you.

When you find yourself getting irritated by someone, examine yourself to see whether you harbor the same negative trait that they're manifesting. This requires delving deep. Usually, you'll find the answer is yes. You likely possess the same trait in some form or another.

Take Emily, for example: She might find herself attempting to converse with her six-year-old nephew. The boy is anti-social, always glowering and scowling at people. He never speaks to anyone. When Emily tries to interact with him, even to smile at him, he scowls even harder.

This prompted Emily to call him a "bad boy," which made the six-year-old even more aggressive. Fortunately, this happened in the presence of some of Emily's good friends who gently pointed out her folly.

Emily turned the spotlight within. Why was the Creator showing her this little boy? Did she also lack respect for others? She realized the answer was yes. The moment this thought crossed her mind, she stopped feeling irritated.

Emily believes that everything has a purpose and that the people and situations we face are meant to teach us something we've been previously unable or unwilling to learn. This understanding has helped her use events in her life to become more self-aware.

Of course, in order to make decisions, you'll also make judgments. They're a necessary part of life. Yes, the boy was being rude, but the most important part of this situation is what Emily was able to gather from it. Likewise, you can use situations in your life to become more aware of yourself.

"Everything that irritates us about others can lead us to an understanding of ourselves."
- Carl Gustav Jung

What to Look For While Developing Self-Awareness

To be self-aware means you're conscious of the following:

Your goals

The events, thoughts, and beliefs that make you happy and sad

Your strengths and weaknesses

Your values and beliefs

Your philosophy in life

Your achievements, how you accomplished them, and what you learned from them

Your failures, how they came about, and how to prevent them from recurring

How you relate to others

How you see yourself and others

Be Aware of Your Motivations

Whenever you do or say something, be conscious of the reason behind it. If you scold a child, ask yourself why. Do you want to assert your seniority or authority, or do you actually want the child to improve their behavior for their own best interest?

"I think self-awareness is probably the most important thing towards being a champion."
- Billie Jean King

WHAT IS YOUR PERSONALITY TYPE?

If you're not sure whether you're an introvert or extrovert, try this simple short quiz online: http://www.nerdtests.com/mq/take.php?id=19

Put simply, the introvert is more prone to self reflection and prefers solitude. He's more interested in his inner landscape. In contrast, the extrovert thrives on social interactions and is highly expressive. He's interested in the external.

Chances are that you, like most people, have a mixture of both personality types. You may express some aspects of your personality in an introverted way and others in an extroverted way.

For example, at work, you may be more of an extrovert, a team-oriented person. You like the energy generated by a group of people working towards the same goals. You may feel uncomfortable and insecure when you're required to work on your own.

On the other hand, during your personal time, you may lean more towards enjoying meditation, reflection, and quiet activities, as opposed to pursuing the adventures of a social butterfly.

Once you're aware of your tendencies, you may want to get out of your comfort zone once in a while to increase your flexibility. In turn, this will enable you to be more comfortable in a diversity of situations.

"The outward freedom that we shall attain will only be in exact proportion to the inward freedom to which we may have grown at a given moment. And if this is a correct view of freedom, our chief energy must be concentrated on achieving reform from within."
- Mahatma Gandhi

HOW TO FLEX YOUR FLEXIBILITY MUSCLE

Step out of your comfort zone with the following exercise:

1. On a piece of paper, sign your name. Notice the feeling of comfort. This is familiar. Maybe signing is even automatic for you.

2. Now write your signature with the other hand. Notice the difference? You'll probably do it more consciously. You'll pay more attention to the process. Does your signature look like the one you created with the hand with which you usually write?

3. Write your signature another six times using alternate hands. You'll probably begin to feel more comfortable when writing with your non-dominant hand. The signature will also begin to look better. If you keep at it every day, you'll eventually be able to write your signature well with either hand.

In other situations, too, practicing a certain way of being or doing things, such as working on a project on your own, will widen your horizon and your possibilities.

Everyone thinks of changing the world, but no one thinks of changing himself."

- Leo Tolstoy

What the Bleep Do We Know?"

This famous documentary made in 2004 marries quantum physics with spirituality. You see how you create your world with every thought. It's a view shared by many quantum physicists as well as spiritual teachers such as The Buddha.

The TV series cites the example of the Japanese Professor Emote's photographs that reveal the transformation of water molecules through exposure to spoken and typed words, music, videos and pictures.

A simple molecule of water becomes a thing of beauty after a priest prays over it. A water molecule from a jar with the word "Hitler" written on it appears ugly.

Imagine then, how our thoughts and words affect us! The human body is about 70% water. This opens up a whole new world of revelation!

According to quantum physics, everything is inter-connected. We are one with everything. We influence our environment.

In the documentary, the protagonist Amanda, played by Hollywood actress Marlee Matlin, begins to transform her frustrated self. She remembers that the human body is comprised of 70% water and thoughts, and that emotion and words affect the molecular structure of water. We watch her becoming a serene, self confident being.

"Men are disturbed not by events, but by the views which they take of them."

- Epictetus

IMPORTANCE OF APPRECIATION

Now that you know that your thoughts influence water, remember to thank your Creator whenever you drink a glass of water. Your appreciation and gratitude will turn it into an elixir.

Appreciate the air you breathe, the food you eat, the people you live with, as well as those you don't see, such as farmers who provide you with sustenance. No man is an island!

Do you see how becoming more self-aware can help you create the life you desire? When you see how you're affecting the world around you, you can transform it to align with your desires by transforming yourself.

UNITY CONSCIOUSNESS

In realizing how all things are interconnected, you've entered into the concept of "Unity Consciousness." Being self-aware includes seeing how you're connected to the rest of the world.

How do you attain this feeling of oneness with all things? One way of doing this is by not differentiating between the Divine and sentient beings. What you do to any of them, you do to the Divine.

"We cannot live only for ourselves. A thousand fibers connect us with our fellow men; and among those fibers, as sympathetic threads, our actions run as causes, and they come back to us as effects."

- Herman Melville

Self-Awareness and the Tao

Taoists urge us to believe in the goodness of our inherent nature, the True Self and the interconnectedness of all things. In Tao te Ching (Power of the Way) the author Lao Tzu, great sage and founder of Taoism, writes: "The great Tao flows everywhere. It nourishes the ten thousand things. It holds nothing back."

In this book, he gives us "three treasures" to help us experience unity with all things:

1. Compassion. With compassion, you don't condemn others for their mistakes, for you recognize these mistakes in yourself.

2. Frugality. The frugal one avoids being wasteful and going to extremes. Living frugally, you can enjoy abundance. Your life will be as simple as your needs.

3. Humility. Humility dissolves the ego and thus removes all possibility of disharmony and conflict. Watch for signs of humility in yourself. True humility revolves around knowing your strengths and weaknesses and being willing to take responsibility for your actions.

"He who knows others is wise. He who knows himself is enlightened."
- Lao Tzu

ACKNOWLEDGE YOUR NEGATIVE TRAITS

Embarking on the never-ending journey of self-awareness requires courage. While it's easy for us to think of our good qualities, our negative traits are often pushed aside. You may even find justifications for your negative thoughts and behaviors. One way to cultivate awareness of them is to look deep into yourself and write down all of your characteristics, positive and negative.

Avoid chastising yourself for your negative traits. Instead, know that everyone is an amalgam of productive and destructive qualities. It's the desire to change what doesn't serve you which distinguishes the self-aware from the deluded.

"You will not be punished for your anger. You'll be punished by your anger."
- Traditional Buddhist quote

PERCEPTION IS THE KEY

Going back to our story of Emily, today Emily has reached a higher level of understanding of the nature of good and bad. She's realized that there is no such thing as good or bad. Everything is an emanation of the Divine. A "bad" situation can become "good" if it's perceived that way.

When Emily found herself jobless, her spiritual teacher suggested she clean the main hall of the temple every day. That would be her new "divine job." Trusting her guru completely, she went to the temple every morning and after sweeping and mopping she would be invited to have lunch with her guru and the nuns.

It was a joyous time for Emily because she chose to make it so. No one who saw her could tell that she was jobless and frustrated. In about two months, she found another higher paying job.

"Your vision will become clear only when you look into your heart.
Who looks outside, dreams. Who looks inside, awakens."
- The Dalai Lama

USING SELF-AWARENESS TO BE YOUR BEST SELF

1. Consider your strengths. This is the fun part. Make a list of your strengths and think of how they're contributing to your happiness and that of others. Some examples may include creativity, initiative, determination, self-reliance and empathy.

    If you find it impossible to list your good qualities, ask a friend or family member to write down what they like about you. This will give you leads, but avoid asking them when they're in a bad mood or annoyed by something you've done!

2. List your achievements. Make a list of ten of your accomplishments in multiple areas of your life. For example, you might list some social achievements, work successes, and achievements in the realm of personal growth.

> Next to each example, write down the skills you used to realize them. For instance, if you went shopping on your own for the first time, what new competencies did you pick up in the process? Maybe you learned navigational skills or discovered that you have good taste in clothes.

Now enjoy your list of accomplishments, skills and competencies. Consider how you can use these in the future. Do you have more than ten accomplishments? Note the others too.

3. Write down your preferences and habits. Maybe you find yourself preferring a certain armchair or place at the dinner table. You probably have a morning routine with which you're comfortable. Maybe you feel out of sorts if you sometimes have to change the routine.

> Sticking to your routine is a great way to beat stress or take the edge off having to make difficult

decisions that take you into uncharted territory. Be aware of your patterns and let go of those that aren't constructive, but don't hesitate to cultivate those that benefit you.

"Knowledge is learning something every day. Wisdom is letting go of something every day."
- Zen Proverb

Resolving Conflict by Becoming More Self-Aware

The cause of conflict is always within us. When you find yourself in an uneasy situation, check whether your ego is in the way. Usually conflict is caused by the need to assert your wishes or the desire to be right. Once you become aware of this in yourself, you can begin to resolve it.

Or it could be that you feel stressed out because of the emotions simmering within you. You may not be aware of them at first. For instance, there could be worry, fear, jealousy, anger, resentment, or frustration, sometimes all at once. At such times, take a deep breath and observe what's happening in your mind. This simple practice will help you to think more clearly.

Everything is based on mind, is led by mind, is fashioned by mind.
If you speak and act with a polluted mind, suffering will follow you,
as the wheels of the oxcart follow the footsteps of the ox.

"Everything is based on mind, is led by mind, is fashioned by mind.
If you speak and act with a pure mind, happiness will follow you,
as a shadow clings to a form."
- The Buddha

KEEP A JOURNAL

Self-awareness entails observing your thoughts and actions. One of the best ways to do this is by writing in a journal every day. If you keep putting it off and allow a week to go by without making notes, you may not recall everything important.

Keeping notes will help you see the patterns and values you've been harboring all along. Once you can identify these patterns, you can begin to change them if they're not leading to positive outcomes.

"I am, indeed, a king, because I know how to rule myself."
- Pietro Aretino

WAYS TO DEVELOP SELF-AWARENESS

When you're self-aware, you learn from your mistakes as well as the mistakes of others.

Here are other ways to develop self-awareness:

1. Adhere to good values. If you have humility, you'll be able to see your mistakes and faults and correct them. You'll also be able to accept criticism. With honesty, you can be open about yourself.

Courage enables you to look within without fear and carry on when faced with difficult circumstances.

2. Read self-help books. Read all you can on the subject and put what you learn into practice.

   Join a community of like-minded seekers. This is an effective and enjoyable way to develop self-awareness. It's easier to polish yourself into a diamond among a community of like-minded people than to go it alone. You may find self-help communities you enjoy online or at your church.

"Your task is not to seek for love, but merely to seek and find all the barriers within yourself that you have built against it."
- Jalal ad-Din Rumi

Your self-awareness will create the life of your dreams. This may not be an easy journey, but it's sure to be interesting and enjoyable. And the rewards are unfathomable.

Conclusion

We're all seeking contentment, perhaps even more than happiness. But we need to view happiness as a side-effect of contentment. The fact is, contentment is a prerequisite to feeling happy. Everyone is driven by the need for contentment.

Some of us seek contentment through achievement or wealth. Others seek it through altruism or creation. Both can be dead ends. Where does it stop? Does a billionaire ever feel content, or does he continuously feel the need to create greater wealth?

Nothing external can ever provide life-altering, radical contentment. Contentment must be found from the inside through kindness, compassion, and self-acceptance.

I hope you've enjoyed reading this Book, but more importantly, I hope you gained something from it. From the very start, I explained to you how destructive a negative attitude is in your life and on your performance. From that, you should realize that no one benefits from negative attitudes and those attitudes can present themselves in many different forms.

That's why it's crucial you remain vigilant and pay attention to your emotions and thoughts. If you fail to do so, you'll open the door for negative feelings and thoughts to transition into a full-blown negative attitude. Once you've taken on a negative attitude, it's harder to get back to the positive.

We then went on to discuss the power of a positive attitude, and how positive traits can combine to form a positive attitude which will help you lead your best life. With a positive attitude, the world is your oyster. You can form the best relationships, perform highly in your job, and achieve happiness that will make you feel invincible.

But, like the bulk of this eBook suggests, you need to put effort into obtaining a positive attitude. Whether you currently have a negative attitude that you desperately want to change or if it's a neutral one that you want to improve, the seven steps we outlined will push you towards your desired goal.

As you embark on the mission to improve your attitude, we advise you never to compare yourself to others. When you judge yourself against others, you'll only bring back those negative thoughts and delay your achievement of a positive attitude. Concentrate on yourself. Then once you have a positive attitude, you can start giving back to all those people that supported you along the way.

No one is telling you it will happen overnight, but with a degree of consistency and an urge to grow as an individual, positive results will arrive quicker than you think. Use this book as a reference tool, if you wish. It's something you can always look back at when you're struggling, something you can read when you lack motivation and something to guide you when you have a clouded mind.

We see people go from being a negative individual full of self-doubt and feeling like an imposter, to a positive person bursting with energy all the time, and I know you're going to be next.

www.ingramcontent.com/pod-product-compliance
Lightning Source LLC
Chambersburg PA
CBHW031625160426
43196CB00006B/280